IDEAS FOR GR
KITCHENS

An overhead pot rack provides both focus and function. For a closer look at this kitchen, see pages 28–29.

Custom touches make a difference. Here, a range-side niche provides a spot for display shelves and decorative prints. Architect: Kirby Fitzpatrick.

Book Editor
Scott Atkinson

Coordinating Editor
Suzanne Normand Mathison

Design
Joe di Chiarro

Illustrations
Mark Pechenik

Photographers: ARX Photography, 84 left; **Richard Barnes,** 6; **Glenn Christiansen,** 71 middle; **Christina del Villar,** 70 top, 82; **Philip Harvey,** 5 top, 50, 51, 87 left; **Grant Huntington,** 4; **Leonard Lammi,** 83 top; **David Livingston,** 80 left; **Stephen Marley,** 60; **Miele Appliances, Inc.,** 79 top, 80 right; **Norman A. Plate,** 71 top; **Kenneth Rice,** 52 bottom, 53; **Showcase Kitchens,** 40 bottom; **Smallbone, Inc.,** 22; **JoAnn Masaoka Van Atta,** 65 left; **John Vaughan,** 30 left, 52 top, 76; **Alan Weintraub,** 58, 59; **Russ Widstrand,** 5 bottom right, 38, 39, 40 top, 41, 62 top left, 69 middle left and bottom left, 71 bottom, 81, 91 bottom, 92; **Tom Wyatt,** 1, 2, 5 bottom left, 21, 24, 25, 26, 27, 28, 29, 30 right, 31, 32, 33, 34, 35, 36, 37, 42, 43, 44, 45, 46, 47, 48, 49, 54, 55, 56, 57, 62 top right and bottom, 65 right, 68, 69 top left, top right, and bottom right, 70 middle and bottom, 72, 73, 74, 75, 77, 78, 79 middle and bottom, 83 middle left and right, 84 right, 85, 86, 87 right, 88, 89, 90, 91 top left and right.

In Pursuit of the Perfect Kitchen . . .

Plot the kitchen of your dreams with this title as your guide. You'll find the latest in both gleaming cooktops and efficient designs. From a cozy armchair, you can examine case studies—18 up-to-the-minute kitchen designs in full-color. Or bone up on European cabinets, convection ovens, commercial ranges, and halogen downlights. If you're ready to dig in, you'll also find a solid introduction to kitchen planning, as practiced by the pros.

Many kitchen professionals and homeowners provided information and encouragement or let us take a look at their new creations. We'd especially like to thank the National Kitchen & Bath Association, Hackettstown, New Jersey; and Nicholas J. Geragi, Jr., of The Room Designer™, East Syracuse, New York. We'd also like to acknowledge Allmilmö Showplace; Bath & Beyond; BK Design Studio; Custom Countertops; Miele Appliances, Inc.; Gene Schick & Co.; Hollis Shaw; and the Northern California Kitchen & Bath Association.

Special thanks go to Rene Lynch for carefully editing the manuscript, to JoAnn Masaoka Van Atta for scouting locations and styling many of the photos, and to Lynne B. Tremble and Barbara Widstrand for photo help in Southern California.

Cover: Graceful curves of cabinets, island, and ceiling soffit lead the eye into this inviting white kitchen. Architect: J. Allen Sayles/Architectural Kitchens & Baths. Cover design by Susan Bryant. Photography by Philip Harvey. Photo styling by JoAnn Masaoka Van Atta.

Editor: Elizabeth L. Hogan

Second printing October 1991

CONTENTS

WHAT'S COOKING?

Super-efficient, flexible, and a little bit of fun—that's the recipe for the contemporary kitchen. More varied than ever, kitchen design features sparkling new colors, fresh styles, and varied components.

Many homeowners appreciate the clean lines and bright colors of the European-style kitchen. Its frameless cabinets, in high-gloss lacquer or laminate, hide efficient aids such as lazy Susans and wire-frame pullouts. Appliances are built in, from refrigerator and microwave oven to the toaster. Even sinks and faucets come in new shapes and colors.

On the other hand, cheery country and traditional styles remain popular. Often the focus of a kitchen is its freestanding range, especially

DESIGNER: SUSAN BRITTON

one of the high-output "residential/ commercial" models. Adding warmth and hospitality are homey accents like potracks, freestanding furniture, open shelving or display soffits, custom backsplashes, and oak flooring.

Open kitchens give a feeling of spaciousness; many accommodate personal options like two-cook layouts, baking centers, or areas for informal entertaining. Popular as ever are kitchen islands and peninsulas, which define the work area yet allow the cook to converse freely with family and friends.

Planning a new kitchen is a threefold process: planning the space, defining a style, and choosing components. You can follow these steps in order or browse freely, using the book as an information source or as a collection of specific ideas to show your architect or designer.

Black European-style cabinets (facing page), granite countertops, rubber flooring, and stylish lighting represent one pole of kitchen design; a traditional "white-and-flowers" great room (below) shows the other. The colorful pullout faucet (bottom left) and modular island cooktop (bottom right) are two of many new components available.

DESIGNER: THOMAS BARTLETT INTERIORS OF NAPA

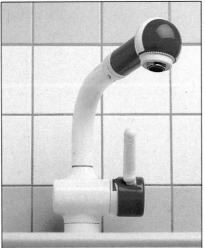

DESIGNER: KITCHENS BY STEWART

5

A PLANNING PRIMER

Sit back, close your eyes, and visualize your dream kitchen. Do images of shiny new cabinets and appliances float before your eyes? Now come down to earth. What's the clearance between the dishwasher and the new island? If you're stumped trying to fit the pieces together, you're not alone.

Use this chapter as a *workbook*, a sequential course in basic kitchen planning. Begin by evaluating your existing kitchen; wind your way through layout and design basics; then finish up with a look at the professionals who can give you a hand.

For ideas and inspiration, peruse the color photos in the next two chapters, examining the case studies of existing kitchens and getting familiar with the latest in islands, downlights, and wall ovens.

The end result? That dream kitchen will reappear, this time on solid ground.

A granite-topped, five-sided island occupies the center of this kitchen, which is separated from existing living space by partial walls of exposed concrete and open-stud framing. Blue cabinet stain and red wall plaster form primary accents to gray and wood tones. Architect: Mark Mack.

TAKING STOCK

First things first: Before the fun of jumping into a kitchen shopping spree, take the time to survey what you have *now*. A clear, accurate base map—such as the one shown below—is your best planning tool. It also helps you communicate with both design professionals and showroom personnel.

Measure the space. To make your kitchen survey, you'll need either a folding wooden rule or steel measuring tape. The folding rule (shown at right) is the pro's choice: it stays rigid when extended and is good for "inside" measurements.

First, sketch out your present layout (don't worry about scale), doodling in windows, doors, islands, and other features. Then measure each wall at counter height. Here's an example, using a hypothetical kitchen: beginning at one corner, measure the distance to the outer edge of the window frame, from there to the opposite edge of the window frame, from this edge to the cabinet, and from one end of the cabinet to the corner. After you finish measuring one wall, total the figures; then take an overall measurement from corner to corner. The two figures should match. Measure the height of each wall in the same manner.

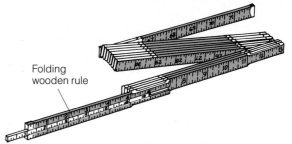

Folding wooden rule

Do the opposite walls agree? If not, something's out of level or out of plumb; find out what it is. Also check all corners with a carpenter's square or by the 3-4-5 method: measure 3 feet out from the corner in one direction, 4 feet in the other direction, and connect the points with a straightedge. If the distance is 5 feet, the corner is square.

Make a base map. Now draw your kitchen to scale on graph paper—most kitchen designers use ½-inch scale (1/24th actual size). An architect's scale is helpful but isn't really required. Some good drafting paper with ¼-inch squares and a T-square and triangle greatly simplify matters.

The example shown below includes both centerlines to the sink plumbing and electrical symbols—outlets, switches, and fixtures. It's also helpful to note the direction of joists (see page 18), mark any bearing walls, and sketch in other features that might affect your remodeling plans.

A Sample Base Map

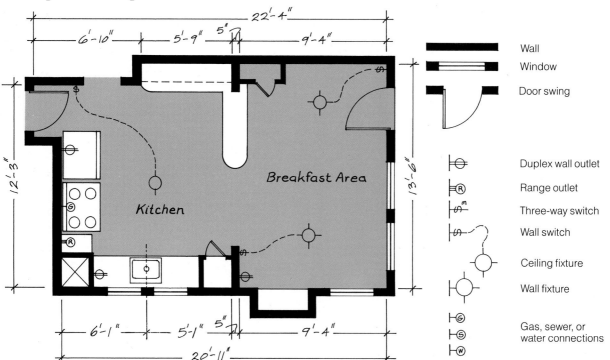

A KITCHEN QUESTIONNAIRE

A questionnaire such as the one below can help stimulate and organize your responses to your present kitchen. When used with your base map, it also provides a good starting point for discussing your ideas with architects, designers, or kitchen showroom personnel. Note your answer to each question on a separate sheet of paper, adding any important preferences or dislikes that occur. Then gather your notes, any clippings you've collected, and a copy of your base map, and you're ready to begin.

1. What's your main reason for changing your kitchen?

2. How many are in your household? List adults, teens, children, pets.

3. Are you right-handed? Left-handed? How tall?

4. Will this be a two-cook kitchen?

5. Do you entertain frequently? Formally? Informally? Do you like great-room (open) designs?

6. What secondary activity areas do you want? □ Baking center □ Planning desk □ Breakfast nook □ Laundry and ironing center □ Wet bar □ Other

7. Would you like an island or peninsula?

8. Can existing plumbing be moved? To where?

9. Is the kitchen located on the first or second floor? Is there a full basement, crawl space, or concrete slab below? Is there a second floor, attic, or open ceiling above?

10. If necessary, can present doors and windows be moved?

11. Do you want an open or vaulted ceiling?

12. What's the rating of your electrical service?

13. What type of heating system do you have?

14. Is the kitchen to be designed for a disabled person? Is the individual confined to a wheelchair?

15. What style is your home's exterior?

16. What style would you like for your kitchen? (For example, high-tech, country contemporary, country French.) Do you favor compartmentalized European layouts or a more open, informal look?

17. What color schemes do you prefer?

18. List new cabinet material to be used: wood, laminate, or other? If wood, should it be painted or stained? Light or dark? If natural, do you want oak, maple, pine, cherry?

19. Cabinet requirements:
□ Appliance garage □ Pullout shelves □ Lazy Susan □ Tilt-down sink front □ Pantry pack □ Storage wall with pullout bins □ Tray divider □ Spice storage □ Breadbox/flatware drawer □ Wall oven cabinet □ Built-in microwave □ Vent hood □ Built-in refrigerator □ Utility cabinet □ Cutting board □ Knife storage □ Wine rack □ Waste basket □ Glass doors □ Open shelving □ Other

20. Should soffit space above cabinets be boxed in? Open for decorative articles? Cabinets continuous to ceiling?

21. What countertop materials do you prefer: □ Laminate □ Ceramic tile □ Solid-surface □ Butcher-block □ Stone □ Stainless steel? Do you want a 4" or full backsplash? More than one material?

22. List your present appliances. What new appliances are you planning? What finish: white, black, matching panel?

23. Would you prefer a vent hood or downdraft system? Do you want a decorative ceiling fan?

24. What flooring do you have? Do you need new flooring? □ Wood □ Vinyl □ Ceramic tile □ Stone □ Other

25. What are present wall and ceiling coverings? What wall treatments do you like? □ Paint □ Wallpaper □ Wood □ Faux finish □ Plaster □ Glass block

26. Lighting type desired: □ Incandescent □ Fluorescent □ Halogen □ 120-volt or low-voltage? What fixture types? □ Recessed downlights □ Track lights □ Pendant fixtures □ Undercabinet strips □ Indirect soffit lighting

27. Consider any other structural additions: □ Skylights □ Greenhouse window or sunroom □ Cooking alcove □ Passthrough □ Other

28. What time framework do you have for completion?

29. What budget figure do you have in mind?

BASIC KITCHEN LAYOUTS

Now the fun begins: it's time to start planning your new kitchen. While brainstorming, it helps to have some basic layout schemes in mind. The floor plans shown below have become classics—practical both for utilizing space and for incorporating an efficient work triangle (see facing page).

One-wall kitchen. Small or open kitchens frequently make use of the one-wall design, incorporating a single line of cabinets and appliances. This is not ideal, as there is a lot of moving back and forth—from refrigerator to range to sink. Still, it's the only choice for some small areas or open floor plans.

An island or peninsula (see facing page) with sink and eating area can provide needed counter space while effectively blocking out foot traffic.

Corridor kitchen. A kitchen open at both ends is a candidate for the corridor or galley kitchen; the design works well as long as the distance between opposite walls is not too great. Traffic flow can be a problem—it's tough to divert kitchen cruisers away from the cook.

L-shaped kitchen. This classic layout utilizes two adjacent walls, spreading the work centers out; typically, the refrigerator is at one end, range or wall ovens are at the other end, and the sink is in the center. The L-shaped kitchen allows a comfortable work triangle; however, now you'll have to decide how to utilize the corner space (see page 15).

U-shaped kitchen. Three adjacent walls make up the efficient U-shaped design (efficient, that is, as long as there is sufficient distance between opposite walls). Often this layout opens up space for auxiliary work areas in addition to the central work triangle—options such as a baking center, a second cooktop and dishwasher, or a complete work center for a second cook.

Great room. A *great room* is simply any large space that houses the kitchen, dining room, and living areas, thus opening up the kitchen as an entertainment space and bringing family and friends together during meal preparation time.

There are potential drawbacks. The kitchen is on constant view and work areas must be blocked out very carefully. Noise can be a problem to consider

Sample Layouts & Work Triangles

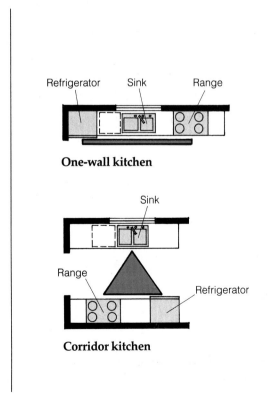

One-wall kitchen

Corridor kitchen

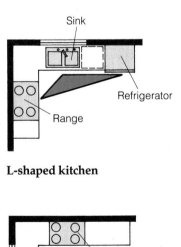

L-shaped kitchen

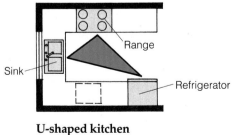

U-shaped kitchen

in great-room design, and privacy is obviously reduced. In remodeling, a great-room layout almost always means knocking out an existing wall or two.

Island. A kitchen island is a popular addition to many kitchen remodels: the extra cabinets and countertop add storage and work space, block off unwanted traffic flow, and can save a cook a number of steps in a large, underutilized space.

On the minus side, islands can cramp space and cut into work triangles and traffic flows. See page 15 for minimum clearance and other guidelines for sizing and placing these units.

Peninsula. A landlocked version of the island, the kitchen peninsula is an effective addition to any basic layout, assuming that there's sufficient room for traffic to move around the end. A well-planned peninsula can augment the work triangle, create a breakfast nook, break up unwanted traffic flow, and corral many storables.

It's sometimes easier to route utilities to a peninsula than to the free-floating island: gas lines, wiring, and plumbing simply come through the adjacent base or wall cabinets.

CONSIDER THE WORK TRIANGLE

Ever since kitchen layout studies in the 1950s introduced the term, designers have been evaluating kitchen efficiency by means of the *work triangle*. The three legs of the triangle connect the refrigerator, sink, and range (or cooktop). An efficient work triangle greatly reduces the steps a cook must take during meal preparation; the ideal sum of the three legs is between 12 and 23 feet. Whenever possible, the work triangle should not be interrupted by the traffic flow.

Today, the reign of the work triangle is being challenged by two-cook layouts, elaborate island work centers, peninsulas, and specialized appliances such as modular cooktops, built-in grills, and microwave and convection ovens.

New studies are under way to bring kitchen theory current with the latest designs. Nevertheless, the work triangle is still a valuable starting point for planning kitchen efficiency. One hint: Sometimes it's useful to sketch in multiple triangles to cover different requirements. If you follow the countertop guidelines discussed on pages 12–13, your basic triangle, or triangles, should fall into place.

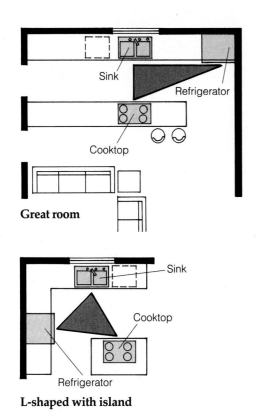

Great room

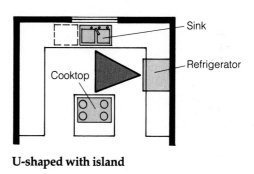

U-shaped with island

L-shaped with island

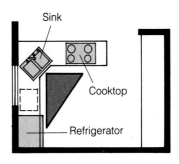

Peninsula

Kitchen Planning at a Glance

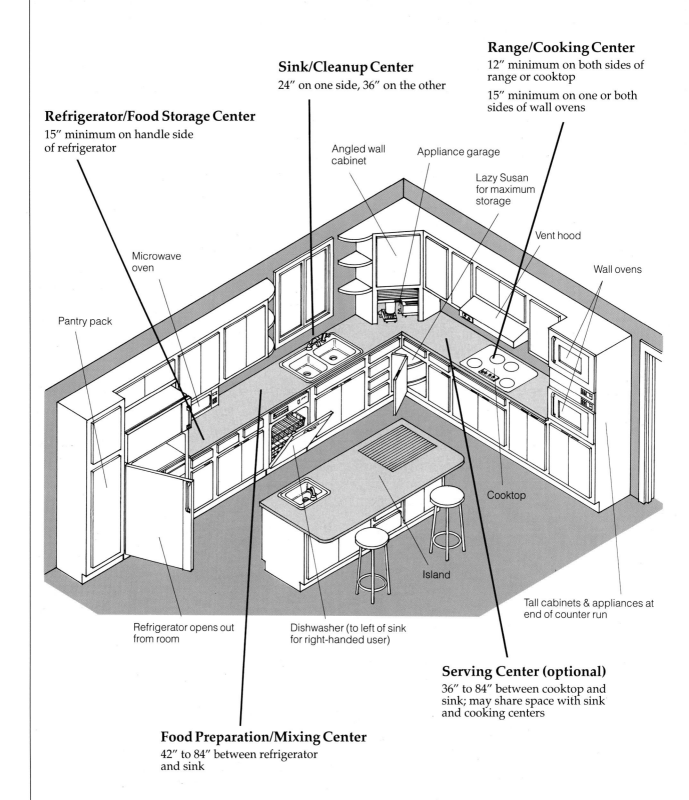

Refrigerator/Food Storage Center
15″ minimum on handle side
of refrigerator

Sink/Cleanup Center
24″ on one side, 36″ on the other

Range/Cooking Center
12″ minimum on both sides of
range or cooktop

15″ minimum on one or both
sides of wall ovens

Microwave
oven

Pantry pack

Angled wall
cabinet

Appliance garage

Lazy Susan
for maximum
storage

Vent hood

Wall ovens

Cooktop

Refrigerator opens out
from room

Dishwasher (to left of sink
for right-handed user)

Island

Tall cabinets & appliances at
end of counter run

Serving Center (optional)
36″ to 84″ between cooktop and
sink; may share space with sink
and cooking centers

Food Preparation/Mixing Center
42″ to 84″ between refrigerator
and sink

MAPPING THE FIVE WORK CENTERS

The real key to planning an efficient kitchen layout is to concentrate on the five work centers, allowing for both adequate countertop space and storage in each area.

Listed below (and shown on the facing page) are guidelines for planning each center. These rules are not absolute, and in very small or oddly shaped spaces you'll need to compromise. Adjacent centers may share space. Corners don't count—you can't stand in front of them.

As a rule, items should be stored in the *area of first use*. The one exception? Everyday dishes and flatware: store them near the *point of last use*—the dishwasher or sink.

Refrigerator/food storage center. Allow at least 15 inches of countertop space on the handle side of the refrigerator as a landing area for groceries. Ideally, the refrigerator is at the end of a cabinet run, near the access door, with the door rotating out. (Need to place the refrigerator inside a cabinet run? Think about a built-in, side-by-side model.)

Also consider an 18- or 21-inch drawer unit (see pages 62–69 for more on cabinets). A smaller unit is too narrow to be useful, and 24-inch or larger drawers will almost inevitably fill up with junk.

An over-the-refrigerator cabinet is a good bet for infrequently used items. Custom pullouts or a stock "pantry pack" are a hit for the tall, narrow spot flanking the refrigerator.

Sink/cleanup center. Figure a minimum of 24 inches of counter space on one side of the sink and 36 inches on the other. (If you're planning a second, smaller sink elsewhere, those clearances can be less.) It's best to locate the sink and cleanup center between the refrigerator and range or cooktop.

Traditionally, designers place the dishwasher for a right-hander to the left of the sink area and to the right for a lefty. But do whatever makes *you* comfortable. Consider the location in relation to your serving center (see at right).

Plan to store cleaning supplies in the sink area. A large variety of bins and pullouts—both built-ins and retrofits—are available for undersink storage. Tilt-down fronts for sponges and other supplies are available on many sink base cabinets.

Range/cooking center. You'll need at least 12 inches of countertop area on each side of the range or cooktop as a landing area for hot pots and casse-roles, and to allow pot handles to be turned to the sides while pots are in use. If the cooktop is on an island or peninsula, the same rule applies.

You also should allow 15 inches of countertop on one or both sides of a wall oven. Typically, stacked wall ovens are at the end of a cabinet run; if they're in the middle, allow 15 inches on both sides.

Although we think of a microwave oven as part of the cooking center, many people prefer it near the refrigerator/freezer or in the serving center. Mount the microwave inside an oven cabinet, on the underside of a wall cabinet, or just below the countertop in a base run or an island.

Plan to store frequently used pots and pans in base pullout drawers mounted on heavy-duty, full-extension drawer guides.

Food preparation/mixing center. This auxiliary center is ideally located between the refrigerator and sink; plan a minimum of 42 inches of countertop, a maximum of 84 inches. Although it may not be a good idea to raise or lower countertop heights (if you have an eye toward resale, that is), the food preparation area is a good place to customize. A marble counter insert is a boon for the serious pastry chef.

Appliance garages with tambour or paneled doors are still popular in this area. (Be sure to add electrical outlets in the recess.) Need a place for spices or staples? An open shelf or backsplash rack provides a nice accent.

Serving center. If you have space, locate this optional work center between the range and sink if possible; size it between 36 and 84 inches (remember, you can share space here with both cleanup and cooking centers).

Everyday dishes, glassware, flatware, serving plates, and bowls, as well as napkins and placemats belong in this area. The dishwasher should be nearby; some models even have integral trays that can be placed right into the flatware drawer.

THREE AUXILIARY CENTERS

Three additional kitchen options have become so popular that they are quickly gaining unofficial work center status: the breakfast/dining area, the menu planning/office center, and the built-in pantry or wine cellar. Before solidifying your plans, think about whether or not you wish to include one or more of these areas.

Cabinet & Appliance Cutouts

To visualize possible layouts, first photocopy these scale outlines and cut them out. Move the cutouts around on a tracing of your floor plan (drawn to the same scale). Then draw the shapes onto the plan. It's easy to make your own cutouts for specialized appliances and other features.

½ inch equals 1 foot

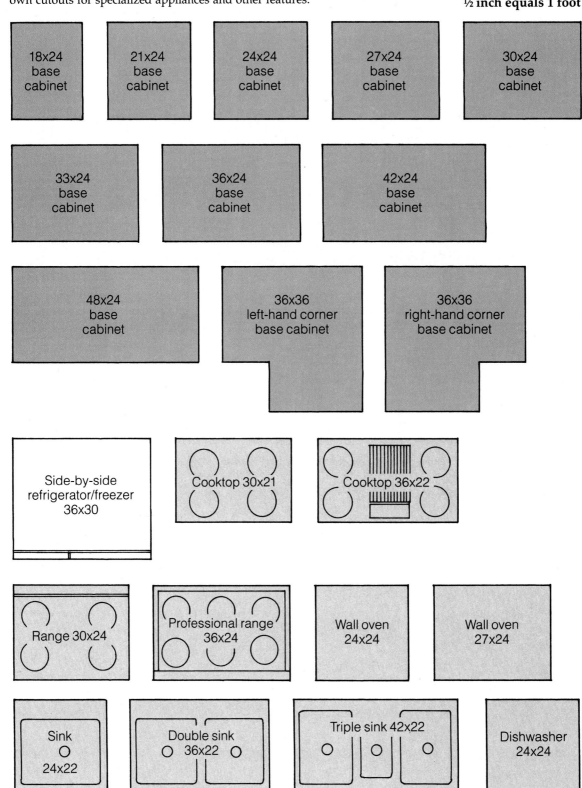

HEIGHTS & CLEARANCES

As shown at top right, there are standard minimum clearances in a well-planned kitchen. These dimensions ensure enough space for both busy cook and occasional cookie monsters; enough door clearance for free access to cabinets, dishwasher, and refrigerator; and enough traffic lanes for diners to comfortably enter and exit a breakfast nook.

Shown at bottom right are standard depths and heights for base and wall cabinets and shelves, plus recommended heights for stools, menu-planning desk, and eating counters.

TURNING CORNERS

Corners are the number one problem when planning cabinet runs. Two cabinets simply butted together waste storage space in the corner: on a base run, this adds up to a 24- by 24-inch waste; above, it's a 12-inch by 12-inch waste.

Angled cabinets, blind cabinets, corner sinks, and lazy Susans all offer corner solutions. For details on these units, see pages 66–67.

WINDOW OVER THE SINK?

The classic kitchen configuration nearly always centered the sink below a window. But how many hours do busy pot scrubbers spend looking out the window? How often is it light when you're working at the sink? Many of today's kitchen designers feel there's no real reason to place the sink below an existing window; on the other hand, consider it. It does bother most people to have the sink near a window but not quite under it.

SOFFITS: OPEN OR CLOSED?

Another decision you or your designer will have to make is what to do with the *soffit* area—the space between a typical wall cabinet (84 inches top line) and the ceiling (96 inches or higher). Should you leave it open? Add open shelves or rails for china and other collectibles? Close it in with framing and wallboard? Extend wall cabinets to the ceiling? Or build a box soffit out over the wall cabinets and add downlights for task lighting? Your soffit choice will help determine the overall look and feel of your kitchen.

Need a crash course on style and design? Simply turn the page.

Standard Kitchen Dimensions

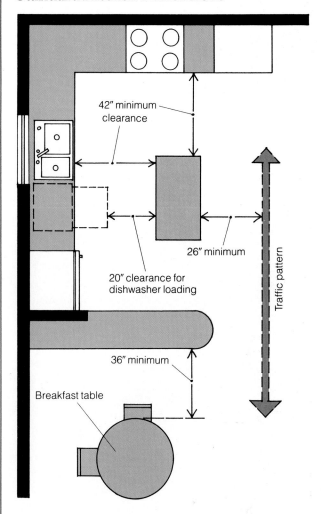

42" minimum clearance

20" clearance for dishwasher loading

26" minimum

36" minimum

Breakfast table

Traffic pattern

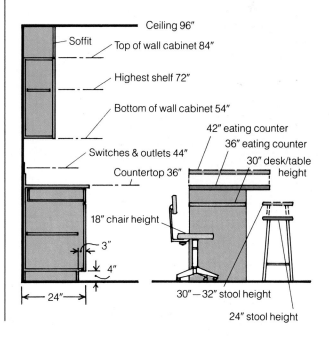

Ceiling 96"

Soffit

Top of wall cabinet 84"

Highest shelf 72"

Bottom of wall cabinet 54"

42" eating counter

36" eating counter

30" desk/table height

Switches & outlets 44"

Countertop 36"

18" chair height

3"

4"

24"

30"–32" stool height

24" stool height

LINE, SHAPE & SCALE

Three visual keys to planning a balanced, pleasing kitchen design are line, shape, and scale. You'll need to consider each of these elements—plus color, texture, and pattern—to achieve the overall look you want.

Looking at lines. Most kitchens incorporate many different types of lines—vertical, horizontal, diagonal, curved, and angular—but often one predominates and characterizes the design. Vertical lines give a sense of height, horizontal lines add width, diagonals suggest movement, and curved and angular lines impart a feeling of grace and dynamism.

Continuity of lines gives a sense of unity to a design. Try an elevation sketch of your proposed kitchen. How do the vertical lines created by the base cabinets, windows, doors, wall cabinets, and appliances fit together? It's not necessary for them to align perfectly, but you should consider such changes as varying the width of a wall cabinet (without sacrificing storage) to line it up with the range, sink, or corresponding base cabinet.

You can follow a similar process to smooth out horizontal lines. Does the top of the window match the top of the wall cabinets? If the window is just a few inches higher, you can either raise the cabinets or add trim and a soffit. If you're including a wall oven, align its bottom with the counter or its top with the bottom of the adjacent wall cabinet.

Studying shapes. Take a look at the shapes created by doorways, windows, cabinets, appliances, peninsulas, islands, and other elements in your kitchen. If these shapes are different, is there a basic sense of harmony? If you have an arch over a cooking niche, for example, you may want to repeat that shape in a doorway, on raised-panel cabinet doors, or in the trim of an open shelf. Or you can complement an angled peninsula by adding an angled corner cabinet or cooktop unit on the diagonally opposite wall.

Weighing the scale. When the scale of kitchen elements is proportionate to the overall scale of the kitchen, the design appears harmonious. A small kitchen seems even smaller if fitted with large appliances and expanses of closed cabinets. Open shelves, large windows, and a simple overall design visually enlarge such a room.

Consider the proportions of adjacent elements as well. Smaller objects arranged in a group help balance a larger item, making it less obtrusive.

RIDING THE COLOR WHEEL

The size and orientation of your kitchen, your personal preferences, and the mood you want to create all affect the selection of your color scheme. Light colors reflect light, making walls recede; thus a small kitchen appears more spacious.

A Sample Elevation

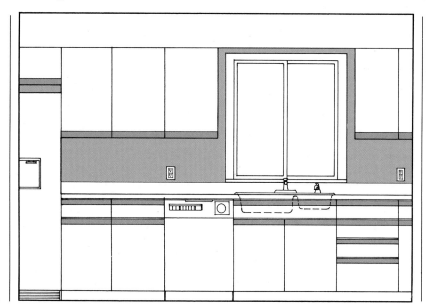

Alignment of vertical and horizontal lines creates a harmonious design. In the sample drawing at left, verticals match up between base and wall cabinets; refrigerator and surrounding storage are incorporated into the flow. A built-in soffit fills the area above wall cabinets and, along with sleek pull bars on cabinets, promotes a smooth horizontal look.

Dark colors absorb light and can visually lower a ceiling or shorten a narrow room.

When considering colors for a small kitchen, remember that too much contrast has the same effect as a dark color: it reduces the sense of space. Contrasting colors work well for adding accents or drawing attention to interesting structural elements, but if you want to conceal a problem feature, it's best to use one color throughout the area.

Depending on the orientation of your kitchen, you may want to use warm or cool colors to balance the quality of light. While oranges, yellows, or colors with a red tone impart a feeling of warmth, they also contract space. Blues, greens, or colors with a blue tone make an area seem cool—and larger.

A light, monochromatic color scheme (using different shades of one color) is restful and serene. Contrasting colors, on the other hand, add vibrancy and excitement to a design; however, a color scheme with contrasting colors may be overpowering unless the tones of the colors are varied. Another possibility is to include bright, intense accent colors in furnishings and accessories that can be changed without too much trouble or cost.

Remember that the color temperature and intensity, as well as placement of any light fixtures, will have an effect on overall color rendition; for details, see pages 91–93.

TEXTURE & PATTERN

Textures and patterns work like color in defining a room's space and style. The kitchen's surface materials may include many different textures—from a shiny tile backsplash to rough oak cabinets or a quarry tile floor.

Rough textures absorb light, make colors dull, and lend a feeling of informality. Smooth textures reflect light and suggest elegance or modernity. Using similar textures helps unify a design and create a mood.

Pattern choices must harmonize with the predominant style of the room. Although we usually associate pattern with wall coverings or a cabinet finish, even natural substances such as wood, brick, or stone create patterns.

While variety in texture and pattern adds interest, too much variety can be overwhelming. It's best to let a strong feature or dominating pattern be the focus of your design and choose other surfaces to complement rather than compete with it.

Designing with Color

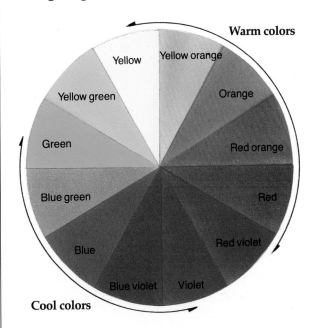

As a rule, work with adjacent colors on the color wheel; save complementary colors—those opposite one another—for accents.

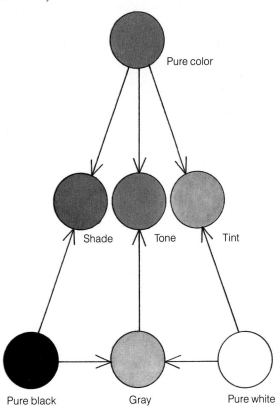

The pyramid illustrates the variation of hues: shades are made by adding black to pure color, tones by adding gray, and tints by adding white. Gray combines pure black and pure white.

Structural Framing

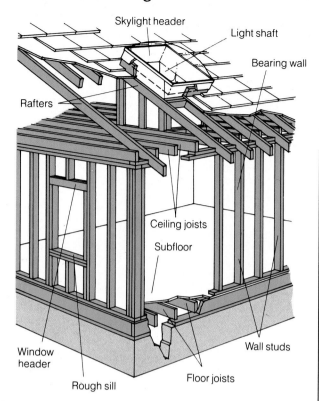

Skylight header
Light shaft
Bearing wall
Rafters
Ceiling joists
Subfloor
Window header
Rough sill
Floor joists
Wall studs

Plumbing

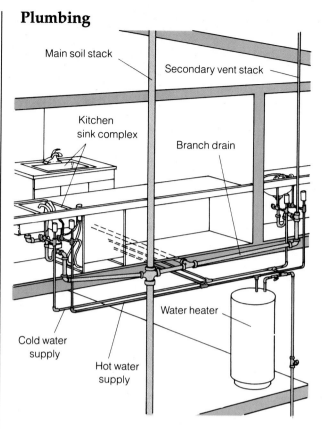

Main soil stack
Secondary vent stack
Kitchen sink complex
Branch drain
Water heater
Cold water supply
Hot water supply

STRUCTURAL CHANGES

Are you planning to open up space, add a skylight, or lay a heavy stone floor? If so, your kitchen remodel may require some structural alterations.

As shown above, walls may be either *bearing* (supporting the weight of ceiling joists and/or second-story walls) or *nonbearing*. If you're removing all or part of a bearing wall, you must "bridge" the spot with a sturdy beam and posts. Nonbearing (also called *partition*) walls can usually be removed without too much trouble—unless there are pipes or wires routed through the area.

Doors and windows require special framing as shown—the size of the header depends on the width of the opening and your local building codes. Skylights require similar cuts through ceiling joists and/or rafters.

Planning a vaulted or cathedral ceiling instead of ceiling covering and joists? You'll probably need a few beams to maintain the structural integrity.

Hardwood, ceramic tile, or stone floors require a very stiff underlayment. Solution? Beef up the floor joists and/or add additional plywood or particleboard subflooring on top.

PLUMBING RESTRICTIONS

Suppose you wish to move the sink to the other side of the room or add a kitchen island with a vegetable sink or wet bar?

Generally, it's an easy job—at least conceptually—to extend existing hot and cold water supply pipes to a new sink or appliance. The exception? When you're working on a concrete slab foundation. In this case, you'll need to drill through the slab or bring the pipes through the wall from another point above floor level.

Every house has a main soil stack. Below the level of the fixtures, it's your home's primary drainpipe; at its upper end, which protrudes through the roof, the stack becomes a vent. A proposed fixture located within a few feet of the main stack usually can be drained and vented directly by the stack. In some areas a new island sink can be wet-vented (using an oversize branch drain as both drain and vent), but this is illegal in other areas. Sometimes a fixture located far from the main stack will require its own branch drain and a secondary vent stack of its own rising to the roof. The moral? Be sure to check your local plumbing codes for exact requirements.

Electrical Wiring

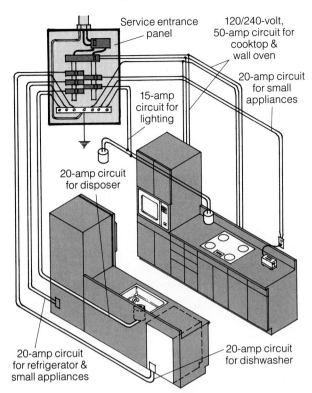

Service entrance panel

120/240-volt, 50-amp circuit for cooktop & wall oven

20-amp circuit for small appliances

15-amp circuit for lighting

20-amp circuit for disposer

20-amp circuit for refrigerator & small appliances

20-amp circuit for dishwasher

Mechanical Systems

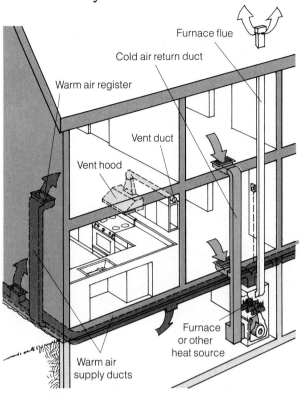

Furnace flue

Cold air return duct

Warm air register

Vent duct

Vent hood

Furnace or other heat source

Warm air supply ducts

ELECTRICAL REQUIREMENTS
Electrical capacity is probably the number one oversight of most homeowners aiming to remodel. All those shiny new appliances take a lot of power to operate! In fact, the typical kitchen makeover requires three to five new circuits.

Requirements for electrical circuits serving a modern kitchen and dining area are clearly prescribed by the National Electrical Code (NEC). Plug-in outlets and switches for small appliances and the refrigerator must be served by a minimum of two 20-amp circuits. Light fixtures share one or more 15-amp circuits, which also run, as a rule, to the dining room, living room, or other adjacent space.

If you're installing a dishwasher and/or disposer, you'll need a separate 20-amp circuit for each. Most electric ranges use an individual 50-amp, 120/240-volt major appliance circuit. Wall ovens and a separate cooktop may share a 50-amp circuit.

Older homes with two-wire (120 volts only) service of less than 100 amps simply can't support many major improvements. To add a new oven or dishwasher you may need to increase your service type and rating, which means updating the service entrance equipment.

MECHANICAL SYSTEMS
Air-conditioning, heating, and ventilation systems may all be affected by your proposed kitchen remodel. Changes will be governed either by your local plumbing regulations or a separate mechanical code.

Both air-conditioning and heating ducts are relatively easy to reroute, as long as you can gain access from a basement, crawl space, garage wall, or unfinished attic. Radiant-heat pipes or other slab-embedded systems may pose problems; check them out. Registers are usually easy to reposition; the toespace area of base cabinets is a favorite spot these days for retrofits. (You can also buy hydronic or electric space heaters designed for these areas.) Don't place any cold air returns in the new kitchen.

Are you planning a new freestanding range, a cooktop, wall ovens, or a built-in barbecue? You'll need to "think ventilation"—either a hood above or a downdraft system exiting through the floor or an exterior wall. The more discreet downdraft system is especially apt for a new kitchen island or peninsula, but vent hoods can add an attractive focal point to some design schemes. See pages 82–83 for more details on ventilation principles and options.

DOLLARS & CENTS

How much will your new kitchen cost? According to the National Kitchen & Bath Association, the average figure is $17,803; in the West it climbs to $22,986. These are, of course, only the sketchiest of estimates. You may simply need to replace countertops, add recessed downlights, reface your cabinets, or exchange a worn-out range to achieve the results you're after. On the other hand, the sky is the limit: extensive structural changes coupled with ultra-high-end materials and appliances can easily add up to $100,000.

As shown below, kitchen cabinets typically eat up 37 percent of the pie; labor comes in at around 20 percent; and, on the average, appliances add another 19 percent. Structural, plumbing, and electrical changes all affect the bottom line significantly.

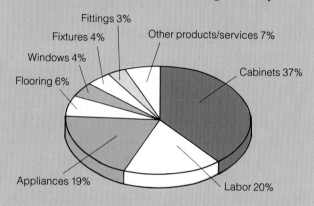

Fittings 3%
Fixtures 4%
Windows 4%
Flooring 6%
Other products/services 7%
Cabinets 37%
Appliances 19%
Labor 20%

How do you keep the budget under control? For starters, know if you're looking at a simple face-lift, a more extensive replacement, or a major structural remodel. Both cabinet and appliance prices vary drastically, depending on whether they're low-, middle-, high-, or ultra-high-end. Shop for ballpark figures in different categories, mull them over, then present your architect or designer with a range of options and a bottom line you're comfortable with.

And what about the cost and criteria for selection of architects and designers you'll work with? Expect to be charged either a flat fee or a percentage of the total cost of the goods purchased (usually 8 to 10 percent). General contractors will work their fee into a final bid. Don't make price your only criterion for selection, however; quality of work, reliability, rapport, and on-time performance are also important. Ask professionals for the names and phone numbers of recent clients. Call several and ask them how happy they were with the process and the results. You may want to ask if you can inspect the work.

WORKING WITH PROFESSIONALS

The listing below covers professionals in kitchen design and construction and delineates the fine points (although there's overlap) between architects, designers, contractors, and other design and construction professionals.

Architects. Architects are state-licensed professionals with degrees in architecture. They're trained to create designs that are structurally sound, functional, and aesthetically pleasing. They also know construction materials, can negotiate bids from contractors, and can supervise the actual work. Many architects are members of the American Institute of Architects (AIA). If stress calculations must be made, architects can make them; other professionals need state-licensed engineers to design the structure and sign the working drawings.

So is an architect the number one choice for designing your kitchen? Maybe yes, maybe no. If your new remodel involves major structural changes, an architect should be consulted. But some architects may not be as familiar with the latest in kitchen design and materials as other specialists may be.

Kitchen designers. A kitchen designer is a specialist in kitchens. These individuals are often well-informed about the latest trends in furnishings and appliances, but they may have neither the structural knowledge of the architect nor the aesthetic skill of a good interior designer (see facing page).

If you're working with a kitchen designer, look for a member of the National Kitchen & Bath Association (NKBA) or a Certified Kitchen Designer (CKD). Each association has a code of ethics and a continuing program to inform members about the latest building materials and techniques.

What about other so-called "kitchen specialists"? (These may include showroom personnel, building center staff, or other retailers.) Some are quite qualified, but some may simply be there to sell you more goods. The decision depends on your scope: if your kitchen needs only a minor facelift, this help may be just what you need; if the job is major, check the specialist's qualifications carefully.

Typically, you provide a rough floor plan and fill out a questionnaire; the retailer provides a finished plan and/or materials list—*if* you buy the cabinets or other goods. Some firms do the work via computer simulation; others the traditional way.

Interior designers. Even if you're working with an architect or kitchen designer, you may wish to call on the services of an interior designer for finishing touches. These experts specialize in the decorating and furnishing of rooms and can offer fresh, innovative ideas and advice. Through their contacts, a homeowner has access to materials and products not available at the retail level. Many designers belong to the American Society of Interior Designers (ASID), a professional organization.

As kitchen design becomes more sophisticated, professionals become more specialized. A prime example is the lighting design field, which has come into its own in recent years. Lighting designers specify fixtures and placement of the lighting for your new kitchen and work with the contractor or an installer to make the new lighting scheme a reality.

General contractors. Contractors specialize in construction, although some also have design skills and experience as well. General contractors may do all the work themselves, or they may assume responsibility for hiring qualified subcontractors, ordering construction materials, and seeing that the job is completed according to contract. Contractors can also secure building permits and arrange for inspections as work progresses.

When choosing a contractor, ask architects, designers, and friends for recommendations. To compare bids, contact at least three state-licensed contractors; give each one either an exact description and your own sketches of the desired remodeling or plans and specifications prepared by an architect or designer. Include a detailed account of who will be responsible for what work.

Subcontractors. If you act as your own contractor, you will have to hire and supervise subcontractors for specialized jobs such as wiring, plumbing, or tiling. You'll be responsible for permits, insurance, and payroll taxes, as well as direct supervision of all the aspects of construction. Do you have the time or the knowledge required for the job? Be sure to assess your energy level carefully!

Warm and woody, or sleek and stark: the choice is yours. At top right, butcher-block tops and copper pots blend with clean white cabinets and classic gas range. Below, unexpected angles, gleaming granite, and slate floor set off ultramodern cabinets and appliances.

ARCHITECT: ROB WELLINGTON QUIGLEY

CASE STUDIES

In the old days, a picture was worth a thousand words. And regardless of the current exchange rate, photos are still the best way to show what's new in kitchen design.

Stylewise, these eighteen studies present as broad a palette as possible. You'll find European cabinets and components, French country motifs, polished colonial brass, high-tech concrete, and stainless steel. But don't worry too much about sticking to one theme: creative kitchens often combine elements of several standard styles.

Each real-life situation is a little different, too. Some of these kitchens are large; others are small. Most of the designs address special problems or requests—hopefully, one of these solutions will work for you. If it's individual pieces that catch your fancy, you'll find more details in Chapter 3, "A Shopper's Guide."

In vivid contrast to ultramodern cabinet layouts, this kitchen sports the "unfitted" look, based on finely crafted freestanding pieces. An ash-and-maple work table commands center stage; stainless steel hanging racks show off their wares; a spacious handpainted cupboard handles pantry chores.

VIEW THROUGH THE ARCH

How can you expand a tiny galley kitchen? To obtain space, this architect first eliminated a small bathroom in back, then added an arch at the entry to the adjacent dining room, and finally opened up the view into the adjoining family room via an angled peninsula.

European-style white cabinets set the tone; curved end cabinets imitate the fluid shapes of the peninsula, soffits, vent hood, and Italian light fixtures. The custom vent hood gleams with polished brass and mirrored steel. Plenty of pullouts, appliance garages, and lazy Susans make storage a breeze—there's even a sealed pullout bin for dog food!

Architect: J. Allen Sayles/Architectural Kitchens & Baths.

The view from the dining room arch (left) includes high-gloss cabinets, blue Brazilian granite countertops, an imposing brass and stainless steel vent hood, and Italian light fixtures that repeat the granite's color. The sink area (shown above) looks out on a soothing garden view; the angled peninsula (right) houses modular gas and barbecue cooktop components and provides a casual eating counter.

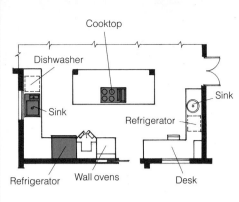

Cooktop

Dishwasher

Sink

Sink

Refrigerator

Refrigerator

Wall ovens

Desk

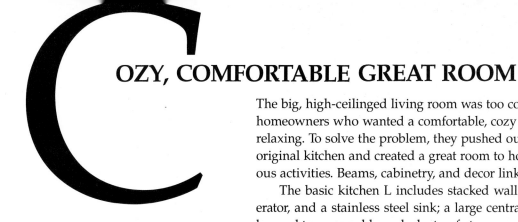

COZY, COMFORTABLE GREAT ROOM

The big, high-ceilinged living room was too cold and formal for the homeowners who wanted a comfortable, cozy space for everyday relaxing. To solve the problem, they pushed out the wall next to the original kitchen and created a great room to house many of their various activities. Beams, cabinetry, and decor link the areas visually.

The basic kitchen L includes stacked wall ovens, a built-in refrigerator, and a stainless steel sink; a large central island houses a modular cooktop ensemble and plenty of storage compartments. Downdraft ventilation preserves the open feel. A built-in desk holds down one corner; a wine bar area completes the picture.

Architect: Remick Associates.

Views from the large central island include a sitting and entertainment area (left) and a window seat and dining nook (above). Custom-crafted, stained-birch cabinets (facing page, top left) harmonize with mahogany floor; solid-surface countertops accent both basic kitchen L and island. Wine bar's hand-painted backsplash tiles (facing page, top center) are a modern match for originals discovered when the old kitchen was torn out.

COUNTRY COOKING

Out went the old walls and in came a new kitchen that meets the needs of a serious cook. The new maple butcher-block island is the center for food preparation; pots on the striking pot rack provide a focal point. A residential/commercial range (insulated for home use) puts out plenty of BTUs; the mirrored wall oven with a pizza insert and the warming tray below complete the cooking center.

The style is clean country contemporary: black granite countertops accent the white, glossy, raised-panel cabinets; the silver and black of appliances add punch. Backsplashes are white field tiles with black diamond accents. Lighting is from PAR downlights with strip undercabinet lighting for close tasks. A new bay window and built-in window seat area complete the far end of the new space.

Architect: Willliam E. Cullen.

The shiny range, wall oven, and warming tray (top) form the heart of the cooking center. Pullout shelves (bottom) make optimum use of "beside-the-refrigerator" space. The tile backsplash (right) matches the enameled cabinets and granite countertops; the glow comes from strip lights behind the wall cabinet valance.

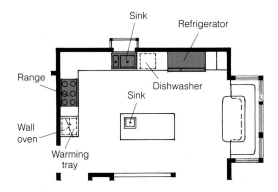

Sink

Refrigerator

Range

Dishwasher

Sink

Wall oven

Warming tray

The kitchen island (below) is the heart of this study in black and white: the butcher-block top provides plenty of surface for food preparation, and shelves hold racks of bulk ingredients and spices. A work triangle wraps around the island; pots are close at hand and provide a striking accent. The rack was constructed from two commercial units.

LIFE IN THE CLOUDS

The arched ceiling and beautiful faux-finished surfaces give an irresistible floating feeling to this kitchen. Glass pendant fixtures lead the eye downward and illuminate the central island.

Cabinets are bleached ash, lacquered here and there for accent. The residential-commercial range is backed with light-filtering glass block and limestone tiles, repeating the limestone of the floor.

Faux-finished cabinets for flatware and glasses line the attached butler's pantry; an additional sink and dishwasher handle major entertaining.

Designer: Agnes Bourne.

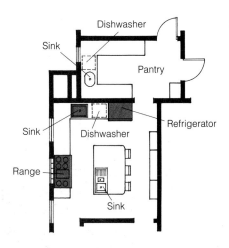

The compact kitchen (facing page) blends bleached ash cabinets with sky-blue and green faux painting and soft limestone. The dark green range (above) has limestone and glass-block backsplash; the original vent hood was repainted to match the ceiling. A butler's pantry (left) has storage aplenty and room to handle serious cleanup tasks.

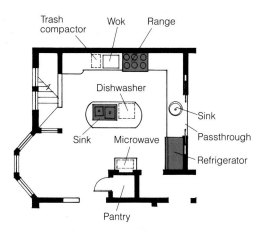

Diamond shapes are everywhere: in the drawer and door pulls; in the range backsplash and vent hood; in the etched-glass wall cabinets and passthrough doors; in the granite-tile counter backsplash; even in the custom glass-and-copper light fixtures.

A STUDY IN DIAMONDS

The homeowners wanted a new, larger kitchen that also had to say *avant-garde*. The kitchen style evolved as both clients and designers started with a diamond motif, liked it in copper, then chose mahogany to complement the copper.

Indeed, copper and mahogany abound. To complete the look, the range area has a shiny quilted-steel backsplash; oak floors have mahogany strip inserts following the island and room outline; walls and ceiling bays are finished with a pale faux-finish paint. A skylight is concealed in one ceiling bay.

But this kitchen works hard, too. At the heart of the cooking area is a professional, six-burner gas range; an electric wok is located just to the left. The large, granite-covered island with its double stainless steel sink is accessible from both cooktop and microwave; the passthrough area has a second sink.

Designer: Osburn Design.

Across the island from the range area, a handsome custom cabinet (right) houses both microwave and plenty of related storables. Etched-glass pocket doors open to create a passthrough to the dining room. Quilted steel and copper set off range area (above top). Granite-tile backsplash (above bottom) has small black tile accents; under-cabinet warm fluorescent lights provide task lighting.

PINING FOR THE COUNTRY

The massive stone chimney was all that remained from a devastating fire; after sandblasting, it became the center around which the new kitchen and living space revolved.

In the kitchen, knotty pine cabinets, strip oak flooring, and bright cobalt blue tiles evoke the country theme. The cooktop area is the center of attention; sink and dining areas occupy opposite ends; and a breakfast peninsula adjoins the sink area.

Pine roof decking towers over all, supported by sturdy beams and iron framing ties. Bay windows at both ends, plus a skylight high in the ceiling, bring in daylight; when night falls, downlights, tracks, and Italian halogen pendants take over.

Designer: Wally Brueske/Design Cabinet Showrooms.

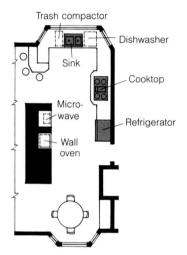

Looking left from the front door, the tiled cooktop area and vent hood (facing page) are the first things to grab your eye. The wall oven and microwave (upper left) are new additions to the massive stone wall; the breakfast nook (lower left) has a cozy, built-in feel and displays a striking pendant fixture. Track fixtures (above) shine down on pine, oak, and an iron pot rack.

LOOKING FOR LIGHT

The owners of this small windowless kitchen had two priorities: first, they wanted European styling and efficiency; second, they wanted to create a feeling of light.

The solution was to combine pale gray laminate cabinets and sleek white appliances, hard-working pullouts and lazy Susans for storables, black countertops, and diamond-accented vinyl flooring. Custom tile work was added for contrast.

As a final touch, these components were mixed with effective lighting: low-voltage mono-tracks and 120-volt downlights for general light, undercabinet fluorescents for countertop tasks, and halogen downlights for punch.

Architect: Suzan Nettleship; general contractor: Iris Harrell.

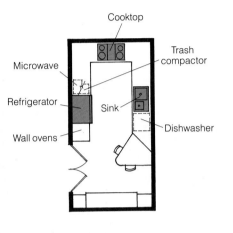

The view over the breakfast peninsula (above) shows the main kitchen, the diamond motif on the vinyl floor, and the cooktop backsplash. The cooktop area (facing page) has a custom stainless hood and modular cooktop; a mirrored storage wall (top left) and etched glass doors (bottom left) lend a light, open look to this small space.

H

OME ON THE RANGE

Cows amble amiably through the wide-open spaces of this Southwestern kitchen. Subdued floor and countertop tiles, plus whitewashed pine cabinets, set the background; the oxydized copper vent hood, island lights, and green cabinet pulls provide gentle accents; handpainted backsplash murals add a dab of primary color.

The custom skylight and a large hanging fixture form the central point around which the kitchen revolves. To one side of the U-shaped layout is the main sink with a window; in the center are the cooking and refrigerator areas; the third side houses wall ovens, an undercounter wine cooler, and plenty of storage space. The island bridges each work center and serves as a breakfast counter; the formal dining table lies beyond.

Designer: Geoffrey Frost/Kitchen Studio Los Angeles.

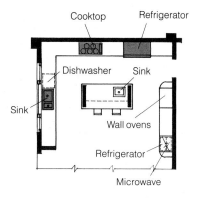

A handpainted tile mural highlights the backsplash area behind the gas cooktop (above); the vent hood and island lamps add soft color. The countertops are rough, French-château pattern limestone with three layers of tough sealer. The flooring (left) mixes Saltillo pavers with diamond-shaped limestone accents.

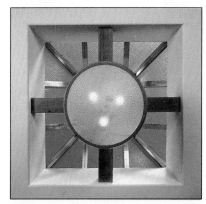

The U-shaped kitchen (below) is augmented by an island with a breakfast counter; the dining table is in the foreground. Day or night, a custom skylight and pendant fixture (right) provide touches of ambient light.

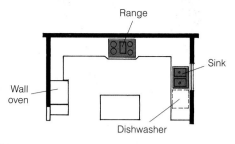

Range

Sink

Wall
oven

Dishwasher

Desk

Microwave

Refrigerator

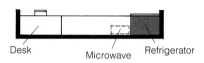

A handy wine rack (left) nestles into the end of the base cabinet run, showing the same attention to detail as the rest of the kitchen. The dishwasher's carved front panel harmonizes with the surrounding cabinets.

VERY FRENCH, VERY MODERN

Curved lines, ceiling beams, and a recurring fleur-de-lis motif are all indicators of the French country look. Here, handcarved distressed cabinets strike the theme; boxed beams, carved valances, and wood wainscoting repeat the motif. Handpainted tiles add color to countertops and backsplash areas; floor tiles are French limestone.

Attention to fine points is also a part of this style, and these cabinets provide great storage and display potential along with their furniture-like detailing. A freestanding island table adds counter space while emphasizing the overall country feel.

The gas range, wall oven, double sink, and dishwasher are all white, the perfect modern backdrop for old-world accents.

Designer: Garry Bishop/Showcase Kitchens.

Handcarved distressed cabinetry invokes the French country style; the main U-shaped area (shown at left) has contrasting handpainted tile on the countertops and range backsplash, plus French limestone flooring. Modern white appliances maintain the clean color palette. The wall cabinet detail (above) reveals several furniture-like touches: curved-panel door frames, a wine glass rack, and slatted dish dividers.

The central island (below) dominates the kitchen; it not only serves as a breakfast bar but integrates smoothly with each work center around the room. Side-by-side 30-inch ovens (left) are located opposite the cooktop; their size determined the width of the island.

TRADITIONAL CHERRY

Frame-and-panel is the style, cherry is the substance, in this well-appointed formal kitchen. Beautiful detailed cabinets provide plenty of specialized storage and house a cornucopia of conveniences: a six-burner gas cooktop with built-in vent hood; an integral-bowl main sink and brass bar sink; matching microwaves; and a built-in, side-by-side refrigerator. White solid-surface countertops add a light-colored accent.

In the center, a massive granite-topped island houses an extra refrigerator, undercounter freezer, and matching side-by-side wall ovens opposite the cooktop. Saltillo tile flooring softens the space and matches the paving on the adjacent veranda.

Architect: MacKenzie C. Patterson.

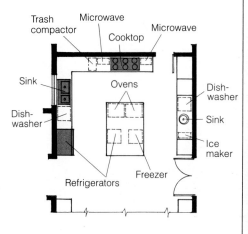

The wet bar area (left) features a shiny brass sink, its own dishwasher, a built-in icemaker, and lots of pullout storage. The main sink area (shown above) features an integral solid-surface bowl, an arched window, and dual appliance garages.

REFLECTIONS IN BLACK

European detailing shines throughout this bold, black kitchen. Floor-to-ceiling cabinets are aspen with semiopaque stain; many coats of clear polyester create the sparkle. Black appliance panels and mirrored backsplash continue the theme—even the existing refrigerator was painted black.

Bullnosed butcher-block countertops, sealed with polyurethane, cut through the black. The peninsula overhang doubles as an eating counter and divides the kitchen from an adjacent dining area. What appears to be strip flooring is really an oak-veneered "floating" system; it's laid over a foam base.

One word of warning: reflective surfaces can require a lot of care to keep spotless!

Designer: Plus Kitchens.

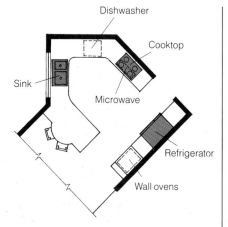

Black aspen cabinets with polyester coating provide the shine; butcher-block countertops and oak flooring add contrast. Kitchen angles provide interest; the lowered ceiling soffits and angled peninsula (right) accentuate the curves. A storage wall (above) wraps around the refrigerator and wall ovens, houses handy pullouts and bins. A low-voltage downlight shows off Italian collectibles inside the glass wall cabinet (left).

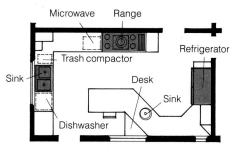

Microwave   Range

Trash compactor

Refrigerator

Sink

Desk

Sink

Dishwasher

OLD & NEW, WHITE & BLUE

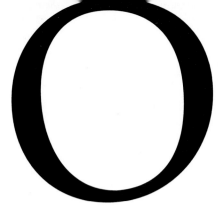

This kitchen's design centered on two basic goals: to skillfully blend the remodel with the existing house style, and to showcase the brand new (but classic-looking) French range. White cabinets have fluting that mirrors the original dining room wainscoting. The blue and gold range and matching hood provide a burst of color; the original leaded glass windows have blue accents as well.

The kitchen's angled peninsula allows for a preparation area at one end and a well-appointed planning desk at the other. The random-plank flooring was stained, then sealed to match the dining room. Discreet downlights provide general illumination; strip lights below wall cabinets add task lighting

Architect: Remick Associates.

New cabinets, peninsula, and appliances blend with existing windows and styling (left). Base cabinets feature custom-crafted fluting, shaped from 1⅝-inch poplar; they support Spanish marble countertops. The kitchen's blue enamel and brass French range (above) has both high-powered gas and electric burners, as well as matching convection ovens. The planning center (facing page, top left) is nestled behind the angled peninsula. An original carved cabinet (facing page, top right) was built into an efficient wall unit.

TIGHT SPACE, EXPANSIVE STYLE

It took some fancy design work to turn this 6- by 13-foot city kitchen into something both visually exciting and highly functional. Bird's-eye maple cabinets, a faux finish, and granite tiles on the floor, countertop, and backsplash provide the punch. A double stainless steel sink and a window fill the short side; the refrigerator, dishwasher, and compact but efficient cooking center—including cooktop, microwave, and undercounter oven—complete the work triangle.

The existing door to the dining room was converted to a passthrough and the arch was added. Miniature track lights provide general illumination; strip lights above and below wall cabinets add both task and accent lighting.

Designer: Fontenot Designs.

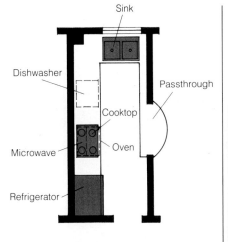

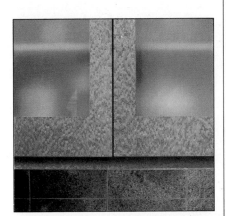

The view through the arch (facing page) highlights the new kitchen. Bird's-eye maple and frosted glass (top left) plus granite tiles provide new life for the narrow corridor (bottom left). The dining room (above) is an ideal spot to view the kitchen; faux finish ties the two rooms together.

A GATHERING PLACE

The family wanted a spot where they could be together—a place in keeping with the turn-of-the-century, formal style of the house. The designer transformed three original rooms into a kitchen, breakfast room, fireplace area, and office—all in one.

The large island defines the kitchen proper and provides plenty of food preparation space; a custom beveled skylight adds interest and brings in natural light. The sunny breakfast area has room for ten diners when the table is extended. Faux-finished walls echo green marble countertops and backsplashes; clean, cheery white highlights the ceiling, appliances, and cabinets. The floors are bleached oak.

Designer: Nan Rosenblatt.

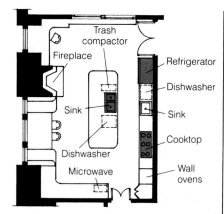

Visible from the island counter, the breakfast nook, or the office, this tile-clad fireplace unifies the kitchen area and offers plenty of room for wood storage. Angles match those throughout the room.

A study in white and green: plentiful natural light beams in on the kitchen area (below) and breakfast alcove (at right); faux finish on open walls and in soffit areas echoes the soft green marble countertops and backsplashes. White cabinets, ceiling, and appliances provide accent and maximize light.

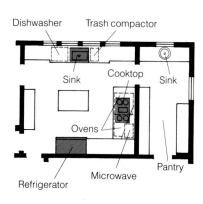

Dishwasher	Trash compactor
Sink	Cooktop	Sink
Ovens	
Refrigerator	Microwave	Pantry

Renovation of existing kitchen cabinets included restoring original brass pulls, clasps, and hinges (left).

NEW LIFE FOR A COLONIAL KITCHEN

White paint, brass accents, and oak floors and trim add up to a classic revival for this colonial kitchen. The designers accepted the double challenge of preserving the integrity of the original design while adding the convenience of modern appliances and fixtures.

Most cabinets are original; others are faithful reproductions. Crown moldings, oak floors and countertop trim, white tile countertops, and lots of white paint complete the room. Modern lighting includes both downlights and undercabinet halogen strips.

The adjoining butler's pantry was a frequent inclusion in colonial houses. Here, the original cabinets have been refurbished; the brass sink and miniature track lights are new additions.

Designers: Bernadine Leach/Kitchens by Design and Nancy Lind Cooper/Cooper Kitchens Inc.

New and old materials combine to refurbish a classic colonial beauty (left). The cabinets are original; the 30-inch ovens, sink, and faucet are up-to-the-minute new. White paint, oak, and additional brass on the vent hood and towel bars round out the picture. The butler's pantry (above) received the same loving care.

COUNTRY ELEGANCE

Although this kitchen means serious business, it's also a visual feast of colors and textures. Everywhere you look there's an elegant touch—a wash of blue, a plastered niche for cookware, a trompe l'oeil cabinet front, the gleam of neatly aligned stainless steel and copper pots. How might you categorize the look? The designers, brought in to help the owners pull things together, call it "French Shaker."

The kitchen has two long, narrow corridors defined by the lines of the sink and preparation table. Nearby is the main cooking alcove, equipped with a professional range, a gas barbecue, and a microwave. The granite-topped island—complete with a second sink and an overhanging buffet counter—continues the center line until the room steps down to a sunny "cafe" area.

Designer: Osburn Design.

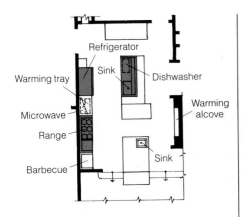

A skylight spills light onto the food preparation area (opposite page, top) and cooking alcove; dark woods blend with light faux-finished walls, stainless and copper pots, and a granite island countertop. The view past the blue-painted, concrete-basin sink area (opposite page, bottom) includes a beautiful clear-finished cabinet.

The wall niche (above) opposite the range and sink is partly decorative, partly for function: a radiant slab warms dishes ready to be served. The dining area (left) has plenty of sunshine, thanks to abundant windows and matching French doors.

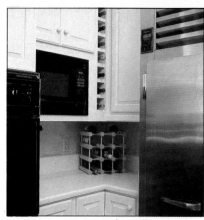

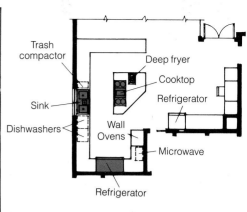

Trash
compactor

Deep fryer

Cooktop

Sink

Refrigerator

Dishwashers

Wall
Ovens

Microwave

Refrigerator

NEW ORLEANS STYLE

Enchanted by the gracious ambience of New Orleans, owners of this home asked their architect to re-create it in their great room. A hammered tin ceiling, arched windows, twirling ceiling fans, and custom cherry units were used to evoke the warmth and spirit of the South.

In the kitchen, a large cherry-and-granite island with modular cooktop holds down center stage; a deep fryer provides firepower for beignets and other down-home dishes. Surrounding the island is a classic white kitchen, featuring raised-panel cabinets and laminate countertops.

Architect: J. Allen Sayles/Architectural Kitchens & Baths.

A solid cherry-and-granite island and towering vent hood (above) hold down the center of this white kitchen; the island style and finish match the living room and dining room pieces (left), emphasizing the great-room effect. The photo on the facing page, top left, offers a peek into the alcove between the wall oven and refrigerator. Between-studs storage space (facing page, top right) was re-created from the original kitchen.

A LOFTY SEASIDE PERCH

This home, which hovers above the rugged Pacific coast, mixes generous expanses of glass, wood, and concrete. The Japanese effect the owner wanted is evident in the natural fir poles, radiating beams, and cedar roof decking, as well as in the open plan of which the kitchen is a part.

In the kitchen area, charcoal-colored laminate cabinets and gray countertops blend with ceramic floor tiles and a massive concrete fireplace rising from the living room below; the island's wood edgings echo both window trim and roof decking. A granite-topped dining table commands the prime fireside location.

Architect: Mickey Muennig.

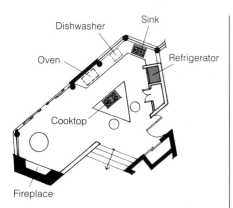

Hardwood stairs lead the eye from the living room up to the open kitchen (facing page), which revolves around a triangular central island and corresponding track fixture (above). The kitchen is bounded on one side by a freestanding refrigerator wall (top left), and on the dining side by a form-stamped concrete fireplace (bottom left).

A SHOPPER'S GUIDE

Frameless laminate cabinets, synthetic marble countertops, batch-feed garbage disposers, halogen cooktops, low-voltage wall washers—enough! The innocent kitchen shopper can be overwhelmed with the latest in gleaming stainless or blaring red components.

What are the current trends in kitchen design? That's where this chapter can help. To keep things simple, we've focused on one component at a time: cabinets, countertops, sinks, appliances, flooring, walls and ceilings, and light fixtures. Color photos show the latest styles; text and comparison charts will give you the working knowledge to brave the appliance center, to communicate with an architect or designer, or simply to replace that dingy old-fashioned countertop.

If you'd like manufacturers' names and addresses for many of the products we show, see the listings on pages 94–95.

The view past a detached coffee bar includes sleek black and stainless components, shiny granite countertops, and both natural and painted wood cabinets, walls, ceiling, and floor. Over the railing at right is the raised breakfast mezzanine. Architect: Remick Associates.

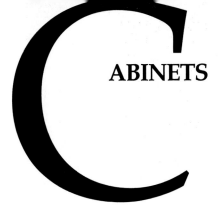ABINETS

Cabinets are the key element in kitchen storage. They create the room's personality and provide the backbone for its organization. For this reason—and because they represent the largest single investment in a new kitchen—it is important to study the many options available before making the plunge.

What materials do you prefer? Your choices include warm hardwoods, sleek European-style laminates, and painted veneers. Will you buy stock cabinets at the local lumberyard, order custom modular units, or have cabinets handcrafted by a custom cabinetmaker?

On the following pages, we show you the two ways all cabinets are constructed and the three ways you can buy cabinets. We also describe the basic cabinet units and how they're modified and organized into a functional kitchen.

Traditional or European-style?

Traditional American cabinets mask the raw front edges of each box with a 1-by-2 "faceframe." Doors and drawers then fit in one of three ways: flush; partially offset, with a notch; or completely overlaying the frame.

Faceframe cabinets offer somewhat more flexibility in irregular spaces than modular ones do; the outer edges of the frame can be

The three cabinet styles on the facing page may look different, but they're all examples of European, or frameless, construction. "Traditional" pine cabinets at top left aren't really frame-and-panel—they have one-piece routed doors. The bright red, curved units (top right) are high-gloss laminate. The maple cabinets (bottom) are truly custom—ebony and mahogany inlays create an accordion effect.

planed and shaped (called "scribing") to conform to unique discrepancies. Since the frame covers it up, thinner or lower-quality wood can be used in the sides (thus reducing price). But the frame takes up space; it reduces the size of the door opening, so drawers or slide-out accessories must be significantly smaller than the width of the cabinet.

Europeans, whose kitchens are so tiny that all space counts, came up with "frameless" cabinets. A simple narrow trim strip covers raw edges, which butt directly against each other. Doors and drawers fit usually to within ¼ inch of each other, revealing a thin sliver of the trim. Interior components—such as drawers—can be sized larger, practically to the full dimension of the box.

Another big difference: Frameless cabinets typically have a separate toespace pedestal, or plinth. This allows you to set counter heights specifically to your liking, stack base units, or make use of space at floor level.

Thanks to absolute standardization of every component, frameless cabinets are unsurpassed in versatility. Precise columns of holes are drilled on the inside faces. These holes are generally in the same places, no matter what cabinets you buy, and components just plug right into them.

The terms "system 32" and "32-millimeter" refer to the basic matrix of all these cabinets: all the holes, hinge fittings, cabinet joints, and mounts are set 32 millimeters apart.

Cabinet Closeups

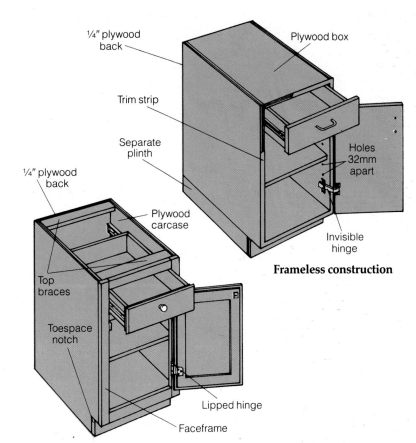

¼" plywood back
Plywood box
Trim strip
Separate plinth
¼" plywood back
Plywood carcase
Holes 32mm apart
Invisible hinge

Frameless construction

Top braces
Toespace notch
Lipped hinge
Faceframe

Faceframe construction

Stock, custom, or custom modular?

Cabinets are manufactured and sold in three different ways. The type you choose will affect the cost, overall appearance, and workability of your kitchen.

Stock cabinets. Buy your kitchen "off-the-shelf" and save—if you're careful. Mass-produced, standard-sized cabinets are the least expensive option, and they can be an excellent choice if you clearly understand the cabinetry you need for your kitchen. As the name implies, the range of sizes is limited.

Even so, you can always specify door styles, which direction they swing, and whether side panels are finished. And you can often get options and add-ons such as breadboards, sliding shelves, wine racks, and special corner units.

Most stock systems also have cabinets that can be ordered for peninsulas or islands, with doors or drawers on both sides and appropriate toespaces, trim, and finishes.

You may find stock lines heavily discounted at some home centers. But buying such cabinets can be a lot

---

COMPARING CABINETS

	Stock	Custom	Custom modular
Where to buy	Lumberyards, home improvement centers, appliance stores, some showrooms (most stock is made in this country).	Few shops have showrooms; most show pictures of completed jobs. Be safe; visit not only the shop but some installations, too.	If you know a brand name, check the yellow pages. These cabinets are mainly showroom items, but some are found in stock locations and department stores.
Who designs	You should, because the clerk helping you order may know less about cabinet options than you do. Don't order if you're at all unsure.	You; your architect, builder, or kitchen designer; or the maker (but be careful; cabinetmakers aren't necessarily designers).	The better (and more expensive) the line, the more help you get. Top-of-the-line suppliers design your whole kitchen; you just pick the style and write the check.
Cost range	Less than the other two choices, but you'll still swallow hard when you see the total. Look for heavy discounts at home centers, but pay attention to craftsmanship.	Very wide; depends, as with factory-made boxes, on materials, finishes, craftsmanship, and options you choose.	A basic box can cost about what stock does, but each desirable modification or upgrade in door and drawer finishes boosts the cost considerably.
Options available	Only options may be door styles, hardware, and door swing—but check the catalog; some lines offer a surprising range.	You can often—but not always—get the same options and European-made hardware that go in custom modular cabinets.	Most lines offer choices galore—including variations in basic sizes and options for corners. Check showrooms and study catalogs.
Materials used	Cheaper lines may use doors of mismatched or lower-quality woods, composite, or thinner laminates that photo-simulate wood.	Anything you specify, but see samples. Methods vary by cabinetmaker; look at door and drawer hardware in a finished kitchen.	Factory-applied laminates and catalyzed varnishes are usually high quality and durable. Medium-density fiberboard is superior alternative for nonshowing wood.
Delivery time	You may be able to pick up cabinets at a warehouse the same day you order. Wait is generally (but not always) shorter than other types.	Figure five weeks or longer, depending on job complexity, material and hardware availability, number of drawers, finishes.	Five to eight weeks is typical, whether cabinets are American or imported, but don't be surprised if they take up to six months. Order as soon as possible.
Installation & service	Depends on where you buy; supplier may recommend a contractor. Otherwise, you install yourself. Service is virtually nonexistent.	In most cases, the maker installs. Buy from an established shop and you should have no trouble getting service if something doesn't work right.	Better lines are sold at a price that includes installation and warranty (one of the reasons price is higher). Some cabinets are virtually guaranteed for life.
Other considerations	You often pay in full up front, giving you little recourse if cabinets are shipped wrong. Be sure order is absolutely correct and complete.	Make sure the bid you accept is complete—not just a basic cost-per-foot or cost-per-box charge.	With some manufacturers, if cabinets are wrong, you'll wait as long for the right parts to arrive as you did in the first place. Check.

Looking for a quick, economical kitchen makeover? Consider refacing. The old kitchen is shown above; refurbished cabinets at right have stained oak doors, drawer fronts, and facing panels set off by granite tile countertops.

like doing your own taxes: no one really volunteers much information that will save you money or clarify your options. If you make a mistake or someone (even a salesperson) gives you bad advice, you're still the one who's liable. Knowledgeable people who can help you select stock cabinets tend to be the exception, not the rule.

Custom cabinets. Many people still have a cabinetmaker come to their house and measure, then return to the cabinet shop and build custom frame carcases, drawers, and doors.

Custom cabinet shops can match old cabinets, size truly oddball configurations, and accommodate complexities that can't be handled with stock or modular cabinets. Such jobs generally cost considerably more than medium-line stock or modular cabinets.

Many cabinet shops take advantage of stock parts to streamline work and keep prices down. They buy door and drawer fronts from the same companies who make them for stock manufacturers. And cabinetmakers are using the same fine hardware (usually German) and tools (multiple-bit drills, metric hinge setters, and precise panel saws) developed for modular systems.

Some cabinet shops specialize in refacing existing kitchen cabinets. This can be an excellent, less expensive choice than replacing the entire cabinet system, with results that look essentially the same as if you had done just that.

Custom modular cabinets. Between stock and custom-made cabinetry are "custom modular cabinets" or "custom systems," which can offer the best of both worlds. They are manufactured, but they are of a higher grade and offer more design flexibility than stock cabinets. Not surprisingly, they cost more, too.

Custom systems offer a wide range of sizes, with many options within each size. A good modular shop can do all but true custom work, using its own components to build a kitchen from finished units. If necessary, heights, widths, and depths can be modified to fit almost any kitchen configuration.

You can change virtually everything on these basic modules: add sliding shelves; replace doors with drawers; set a matching hood unit over the stove; add wire baskets, flour bins, appliance garages, and pullout pantries.

Though frameless modular cabinets are sized metrically (standard depth is 60 centimeters—about 24 inches), nearly all lines are now sized for American appliances.

One thing agreed upon by modular retailers and custom shops alike is that frameless cabinets will replace faceframe ones as the dominant style. "At this point, faceframe is largely a look; it can be duplicated in frameless," one cabinetmaker told us.

Wall Cabinet Options

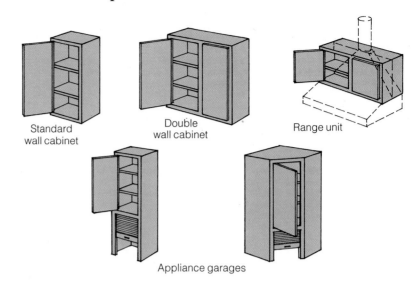

Wall cabinets come in singles, doubles, and various specialty configurations. Typically 12 or 15 inches deep, cabinets can vary in width from 9 to 60 inches. Although the most frequently used heights are 15, 18, and 30 inches, units range from 12 to 36 inches high, and even taller.

Standard wall cabinet

Double wall cabinet

Range unit

Appliance garages

What options are available?

The illustrations on these two pages show many of your basic cabinet choices; you'll find variations on these units in most cabinet lines.

Perhaps more options exist for corners than for any other kitchen cabinet space. The simplest corner butts one cabinet against another, providing inconvenient access to the corner. Better options include angled units with larger doors, double-door units that provide full access to the L-shaped space, and lazy Susans or other slide-out accessories that bring items from the back up to the front.

Hardware options are available to add to the versatility of kitchen cabinets. For examples, see page 69.

Judging quality

To determine the quality of a cabinet, look closely at the drawers; they take more of a beating than any other part of your cabinets. "Drawers are a cabinet within a cabinet," says one maker. "They tell all." Compare drawers in several lines, examining the joinery in each, and you'll begin to see differences.

Drawer guides and cabinet hinges are the critical hardware elements. Check for adjustability of both; they should be able to be reset and fine-tuned with the cabinets in place. Some frameless cabinets also have adjustable mounting hardware, so you can relevel them even after they're hanging on the wall.

Determine whether drawer guides allow full or only partial ex-

Base Cabinet Options

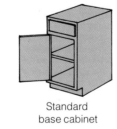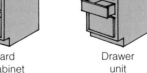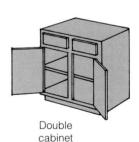

Standard base cabinet

Drawer unit

Double cabinet

When complete with a toespace or plinth, base cabinets normally measure 34½ inches tall; the counter adds another 1½ inches. In width, they range from 9 to 60 inches, increasing in increments of 3 inches from 9 to 36 inches and increments of 6 inches after that. Standard depth is 24 inches.

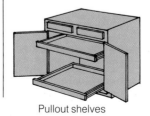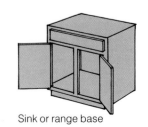

Pullout shelves

False sink front

Sink or range base

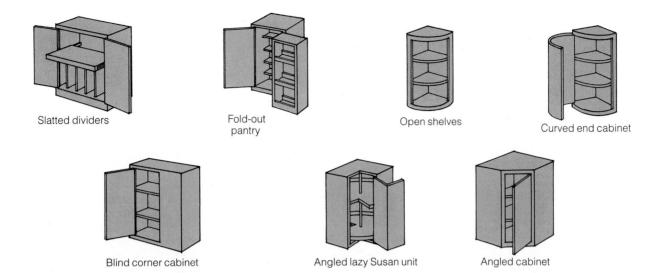

Slatted dividers

Fold-out pantry

Open shelves

Curved end cabinet

Blind corner cabinet

Angled lazy Susan unit

Angled cabinet

tension of drawers. Check to see that doors and drawers align properly.

Make sure laminate and edge banding are thick enough not to peel at the corners and edges. "Once they start peeling on a cheap cabinet, that's it," one shop warned.

Getting help

The cabinets are only part of the puzzle. When you buy cabinets, some of what you're paying for is varying degrees of help with the design.

A designer will help you figure out how you'll use the kitchen. Some retailers will give you a questionnaire (much like the one on page 9) to find out what's wrong with your current kitchen, how often you do any specialty cooking, whether your guests always end up in the kitchen, whether you buy food in bulk, and other helpful clues to the final design solution.

Pick a "look," then shop for it; compare features, craftsmanship, budget, and cost. Some designers

represent a particular line, so shop around to get an idea of what's currently available.

Your current floor plan (see page 8) is the best aid you can offer a designer. Some staff designers in showrooms will do the new cabinet plan for you, applying the charge against the purchase price of the cabinets. Some showrooms even use computer renderings to help customers visualize the finished kitchen—and prices for different cabinets are just a keystroke away.

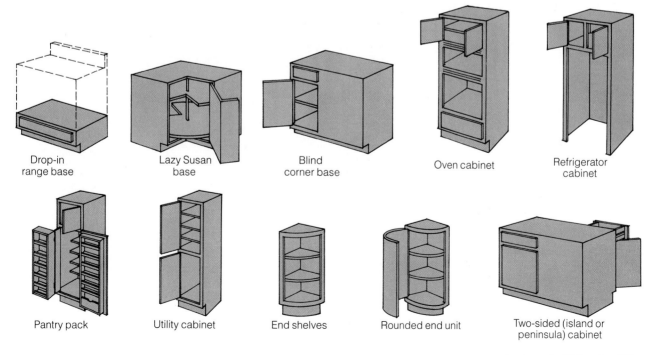

Drop-in range base

Lazy Susan base

Blind corner base

Oven cabinet

Refrigerator cabinet

Pantry pack

Utility cabinet

End shelves

Rounded end unit

Two-sided (island or peninsula) cabinet

ARCHITECT: WILLIAM TURNBULL

Island cabinets utilize wasted floor space, define traffic patterns, and offer valuable preparation and storage space. A formal, handcarved island (above) divides the long corridor kitchen and augments cooking and cleanup centers. The freestanding table island (right) adds a furniture-like touch, providing movable counter space where it's needed.

ARCHITECT: COSTARELLA ARCHITECTS

And what will all this cost?

There are no figures after "Cost range" in the chart on page 64. Why? Because so many factors influence the final price. The kitchens you see on these pages have cabinets that range from about $400 to more than $80,000.

The wide range of styles—and prices—makes buying cabinets much like buying a car. Like car makers, every manufacturer or cabinetmaker picks a slot of the market, then offers various styles and options that raise or lower the basic price. If you're looking for the cabinet equivalent of "transportation," you can pay a lot less than someone looking for something sportier.

Know your budget. You'll quickly find out what kinds of cabinets you can afford; with your plan in hand, you can get a basic price for standard cabinets relatively easily. But options will drastically alter the quote—so the same basic cabinet can end up costing a lot of different prices. Bids should be full quotes based on a fully specified room sketch listing the options desired in each cabinet.

Within each line, basic costs are determined by the wood species and the style of the doors and drawers. Remember, the basic frame carcase will be the same within a line no matter what door style you choose.

Even if you're favoring manufactured cabinets, consider including a bid from a custom shop for comparison. As with stock and custom modular bids, make sure your plan is specific enough to get a reliable quote. Ask for complete shop drawings, so there's no misunderstanding as to what you're ordering.

An explosion of new hardware products awaits the cabinet shopper. Shown clockwise, from top right: swiveling spice rack; corner base lazy Susan; adjustable pullout shelf; sink unit with tilt-down front and specialty units; pantry pack's pivoting, pullout wire shelves.

COUNTERTOPS

Chop on it, knead on it, serve from it: you ask a lot, every day, of your kitchen countertop. No one material is best for all purposes, but each of the six described below looks distinctive and has specific advantages.

What are your choices?

Any one of these six surfaces can be installed throughout your kitchen. But you might want to consider a combination, placing heat-resistant materials near the stove, easy-cleanup surfaces near the sink, a cool stone insert where it's handy for dough preparation.

The problem is that you probably won't find all the materials in the same place. Some dealers with showrooms are listed in the yellow pages under Kitchen Cabinets &

COMPARING COUNTERTOPS

DESIGNER: BERNADINE LEACH

Plastic laminate

Advantages. You can choose from a wide range of colors, textures, and patterns. Laminate is durable, easy to clean, water-resistant, and relatively inexpensive. With the right tools, you can install it yourself.

Disadvantages. It can scratch, scorch, chip, and stain, and it's hard to repair. Conventional laminate has a dark backing that shows at its seams; new solid-color laminates, designed to avoid this, are somewhat brittle and more expensive.

Cost. Standard brands cost $1 to $3.50 a square foot; premolded, particleboard-backed tops in limited colors are $5 to $10 per running foot. Installed, a custom countertop with 2-inch lip and low backsplash costs from $40 to $90 per running foot (more for solid-color materials).

Ceramic tile

Advantages. It's good-looking, comes in many colors, textures, and patterns, is heat-proof, scratch-resistant, and water-resistant if installed correctly. Grout is also available in numerous colors. Patient do-it-yourselfers are likely to have good results.

Disadvantages. Many people find it hard to keep grout satisfactorily clean. Some kitchen designers recommend using less grout space ($\frac{3}{32}$ inch versus the typical $\frac{1}{4}$ inch), but the thinner joint is definitely weaker. You can also buy grout sealers, but their effectiveness is disputed. Hard, irregular surface can chip china and glassware. High-gloss tiles show every smudge.

Cost. Prices range from 50 cents to $50 per square foot. Choose nonporous glazed tiles, which won't soak up spills and stains. Installation costs vary, depending on tile type and size of job (generally, the smaller the countertop, the higher the per-foot price).

DESIGNER: ESTHER H. REILLY

Solid-surface

Advantages. Durable, water-resistant, heat-resistant, nonporous, and easy to clean, this marble-like material can be shaped and installed with woodworking tools (but do it very carefully, or cracks can occur, particularly around cutouts). It allows for a variety of sink installations, including an integral unit like the one shown on page 74. Blemishes and scratches can be sanded out.

Disadvantages. It's expensive, and requires very firm support below. Until recently, color selection was limited to white, beige, and almond; now imitation stone and pastels are common.

Cost. For a 24-inch-deep counter with a 2-inch front lip and 4-inch backsplash, figure $100 to $150 per running foot, installed. Uninstalled it's about half that. Costs go up for wood inlays and other fancy edge details.

Equipment; they'll probably have tile, plastic laminate, solid-surface, and—maybe—wood. Larger building supply centers and lumberyards usually carry plastic laminate and wood. For the appropriate dealer or fabricator, check listings in the categories Marble—Natural, Plastics, Restaurant Equipment, Sheet Metal Work, and Tile. Kitchen designers, interior designers, and architects can also supply samples of countertop materials.

What experts say

The chefs, designers, and architects we spoke with did not agree on any single surface.

Chefs preferred stainless steel, granite, marble, or—if it could be kept sanitary—wood. Designers and architects agreed with them, to a point. Restaurant kitchens are decidedly different in three ways: they aren't designed to be aesthetically pleasing; they put far greater de-

mands on each work surface; and they're not usually places to economize, given the need for extreme durability.

Residential designers take a more realistic approach. Although homeowners might jump at the prospect of granite countertops, the cost is prohibitive for many. But, as one dealer told us, "You can combine materials to make a little piece of a really choice one go a long way—perhaps spend a lot on a small section of

---

COMPARING COUNTERTOPS

Wood

Advantages. Wood is handsome, natural, easily installed, and easy on glassware and china.

Disadvantages. It's harder to keep clean than nonporous materials. It can scorch and scratch, and it may blacken when near a source of moisture. You can seal it with mineral oil, but seal both sides or the counter may warp. It's a good idea to make an insert (or even the countertop itself) removable for easy cleaning or resurfacing. Or use a permanent protective sealer, such as polyurethane (but then you can't cut on it).

Cost. Maple butcher-block, the most popular, costs about $12 to $16 per square foot for 1½- to 1¾-inch thickness. Installed cost is $50 and up per running foot, including miters and cutouts. It's sold in 24-, 30-, and 36-inch widths. Smaller pieces are available for inserts. Oak, sugar pine, and birch are also used for counters.

Stainless steel

Advantages. Stainless steel is waterproof, heat-resistant, easy to clean, seamless, and durable. You can get a counter with a sink molded right in. It's great for a part of the kitchen where you'll be using water a lot.

Disadvantages. Don't cut on it, or you risk damaging both countertop and knife. Fabrication is expensive; you can, however, reduce the cost by using flat sheeting and a wood edge, as in the counter shown at right.

Cost. The price of 16-gauge stainless (about ¹⁄₁₆ inch thick) is about $5.50 per square foot, just for material. For sink cutouts, faucet holes, and bends and welds for edges and backsplashes, count on about 3 to 6 hours' fabrication time at about $45 per hour for an installed 6- to 10-foot-long counter. Custom detailing and high-chromium stainless up the price—as high as $300 to $500 per running foot.

Stone

Advantages: Granite and marble, both used for countertops, are beautiful natural materials. Their cool surface is very helpful when you're working with dough or making candy. They're heatproof, water-resistant, easy to clean, and very durable.

Disadvantages. Oil, alcohol, and any acid (such as those in lemons or wine) will stain marble or damage its high-gloss finish; granite can stand up to all of these. Solid slabs are very expensive; recently, some homeowners and designers have turned to stone tiles—including slate and limestone—as less expensive alternatives.

Cost. A custom-cut marble slab costs $40 to $70 per square foot, granite about $60 and up—polished and finished with a square or slightly beveled edge. Decorative edge details and the like add more. Marble counter inserts run $30 to $45 per square foot. Installation costs about $75 an hour.

Backsplashes, the areas above countertops or behind range or cooktop, are favorite spots for decoration. The wine-country kitchen below sports custom wine-label accent tiles above a solid-surface countertop. A Mexican kitchen's cooktop area (right) is a feast of handpainted tile.

DESIGNER: WALLY BRUESKE/DESIGN CABINET SHOWROOMS

ARCHITECT: SHAKESPEARE & BURNS

marble, but make up for it with a large section of less expensive laminate—and still get the benefits of both surfaces."

Backsplash fever

These days, countertops aren't the only area where designers are making a fashion statement; the backsplash—the wall surface between the countertop proper and the wall cabinets overhead—is now artistically in vogue as well. (This area usually stretches for about 18 vertical inches—from 36 to about 54 inches from the floor.) The wall behind a freestanding range or cooktop is another model for design; there's usually more room there for a special statement. A good backsplash also has a practical side: if properly installed, it seals this vulnerable area from moisture penetration, and it makes the wall a lot easier to keep clean.

Just a few years ago, the average countertop, usually laminate, included a 4-inch lip on the back. Today's higher backsplashes, however, often feature materials that are found there alone. Geometric tile patterns and handpainted accent tiles are favorite choices. Stone tiles are an economical alternative to solid granite or marble (for visual spark, try laying these 8- or 12-inch squares on the diagonal). Even stainless steel and mirrored surfaces are showing up in high-tech surroundings. Under-cabinet strip lights (see pages 91–93) can add drama, too.

Need more inspiration? The photos in Chapter 2 present a wide variety of backsplash treatments.

SINKS & FITTINGS

The cleanup center is the number one command post of nearly every busy kitchen; in fact, studies claim that up to 50 percent of kitchen time is spent there. So doesn't it make sense to pay special attention to sinks, faucets, and related accessories when you're planning your new kitchen?

Recently, sinks and faucets have become prime design accents—an imaginative way to add a splash of color to an otherwise restrained design scheme. And if you later decide you don't like the boldness, it's a lot easier to change a sink or faucet than your kitchen cabinets!

The new world of sinks

When it comes to main kitchen sinks, the single-bowl version is mostly a thing of the past. Today's sink is a multitask center, and double-, even triple-bowl designs are now the norm. They come detailed with many custom-fitted accessories, such as cutting boards, colanders, rinsing baskets, and dish racks.

Sink color is a new realm, too: white and stainless are still tops, but red, black, and a rainbow of other designer tones are on the scene, too. Colored bowl strainers and accessories are also available.

Materials. Common sink materials include stainless steel, enameled cast iron or steel, vitreous china, brass, and copper.

■ *Stainless steel.* Stainless steel sinks come in 18- or 20-gauge (18-gauge is stronger) and either matte or mirror finish. Chromium/nickel blends—such as Type 302 stainless—are tops. These are the only true "stainless" sinks; cheaper grades will stain. Matte finishes are much easier to keep looking clean than mirrored, and they mask scratches better.

Stainless is relatively noisy; look for a sink with an undercoating. Integral drain boards are available, too.

■ *Enameled cast iron/steel.* Here's where the colors come in. These sinks are gaining in popularity, especially with the advent of new European designs. Black, gray, and a palette of other colors and flecked patterns are available. Enameled cast-iron sinks have a heavier layer of baked-on enamel than steel, making them qui-

ARCHITECT: J. ALLEN SAYLES

eter and less likely to chip, but also more expensive.

■ *Quartz.* A new, expensive import from Europe, quartz sinks look similar to enamel but stand abuse better and are easier to clean.

■ *Vitreous china.* Vitreous china sinks, a common bathroom component, are starting to show up in the kitchen. These are highly ornamental, sculpted sinks but very expensive.

■ *Integral solid-surface sinks.* Today's solid-surface countertops (see page 70) can be coupled with a molded, integral sink for a sleek, sculpted look. Sink color can either

Sinks are more stylish and functional than ever. Sleek vitreous china sink (top right) is a newcomer, features strainer and chopping board inserts; stainless steel models, such as triple-bowl model with dish rack and strainer (bottom right), are still most popular. Bar sink (top) shows off its bright brass punch.

match the countertop exactly or complement it—for example, you might choose a cream-colored sink below a granite-colored top. Edge-banding and other border options abound. Although they're not indestructible, solid-surface sinks can be repaired if nicked or scratched.

■ *Brass and copper sinks.* These strikingly elegant surfaces are outstanding as accents. However, they require zealous maintenance, so you'll probably want to reserve them for wet-bar or other occasional uses. Bar or hospitality sinks come with either a 2- or 3½-inch drain opening; if you're planning to add a disposer you'll want the larger opening.

Rim or no rim? You also have a choice of mounting methods with various sink models. *Self-rimming* sinks with molded overlaps are supported by the edge of the countertop cutout; *flush* deck-mounted sinks have surrounding metal strips to hold the basin to the countertop; *unrimmed* sinks are recessed under the countertop and held in place by metal clips.

Faucets

Today's kitchen faucets fall into one of two camps: Euro-sophistication or traditional. Enameled single-lever fixtures with pullout sprayers and in-

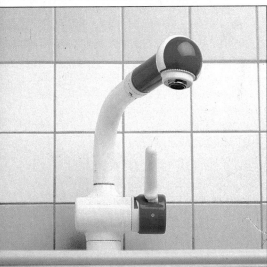

How about a seamless, solid-surface sink? The one above is white-on-white, with decorative grooving and adjacent drainboard; other models have contrasting sink colors or border designs.

Like sinks, faucets are now design accents—they come in a rainbow of choices. The traditional brass gooseneck model (top left) is popular for country kitchens; single-lever European styles (middle and bottom left) offer bright colors, interchangeble attachments, and pullout sprayers.

terchangeable attachments are fashionable, but traditional brass or chrome gooseneck styles with individual handles remain popular, too. Whatever you choose, most kitchen professionals agree that solid-brass construction is the way to go.

When you select your sink, be sure the holes in it will accommodate the type of faucet you plan to buy as well as any additional accessories.

Garbage disposers

Today's garbage disposers handle almost all types of food waste. They come in two types: batch-feed and continuous. Batch-feed disposers kick into gear when you engage the lid; continuous-feed models are activated by an adjacent wall switch.

Look for sturdy motors (½ horsepower or more), noise insulation, and antijam features. Generally, the fatter the disposer, the more the insulation—and the quieter it's likely to run.

Hot & cold water dispensers

Half-gallon-capacity instant hot water dispensers have been around for some time now. The heater fits underneath the sink (see drawing below); connected to the cold water supply, it delivers 190° to 200°F water. Most units plug into a 120-volt grounded outlet installed inside the sink cabinet. Mount the dispenser spout either on a sink knockout or nearby on the countertop.

Cold water spouts operate in a similar manner, but a below-counter chiller is substituted for the heater.

Water purifiers

New compact water purifiers look just like hot water or soap dispensers on the sink; the main unit fits compactly underneath the sink like other water appliances. Look for a government approval seal and easy-to-change filter cartridges.

Hot-water dispenser, providing 190° to 200F° water on demand, is a common inhabitant of modern kitchens. Mount the spout on the sink or adjacent countertop; the tank resides below-deck.

The drawing at right shows the mysterious underworld of today's kitchen sink, where fittings and pipes abound. Dishwasher and garbage disposer link with the sink drain; both the dishwasher and hot water dispenser tap into supply lines on the way to the faucet. Electrical connections may be either plug-in or hard-wired; be sure your circuit capacity is up to local codes.

Inside the Sink Complex

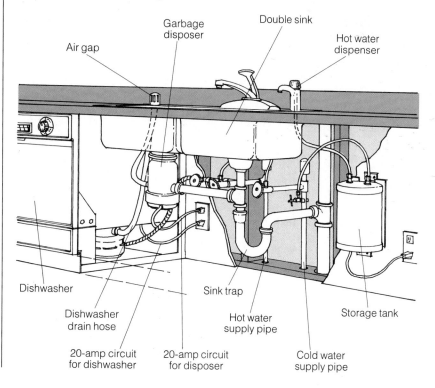

DESIGNER: OSBURN DESIGN

RANGES

What's best, the flexibility of separate cooktops and ovens or the traditional integrated range? On one level, the choice is one of function. But in addition to that, it's a question of style: the range creates a focal point, invoking the traditional image of "hearth and home."

Freestanding, slide-in, or drop-in?

Take your choice of three types of ranges: freestanding, slide-in (freestanding without side panels to fit between cabinets), and drop-in. Most ranges have a cooktop with oven below; a few models offer an additional upper microwave oven with a built-in ventilator or downventing cooktop. Standard range width is 30 inches, but sizes go as narrow as 21 inches and, in commercial designs, as wide as 48 inches or more.

Which style is for you?

Choose from standard models—gas or electric, commercial units, or new residential/commercial. For a discussion of burner options, see pages 78–79; for oven specifics, turn to pages 80–81.

■ *Electric ranges* may have standard coils, solid-element burners, or a smooth ceramic top, plus radiant-heat or convection/radiant ovens.

■ *Gas ranges* have either radiant-heat or convection ovens; lower ovens may be self-cleaning or continuous-cleaning. Some models offer interchangeable modules.

■ *Commercial gas units* have been a "hot" item in recent years—partly due to increased BTU output, partly because of their look of "serious business." Their performance is excellent, but they create many problems for home use: they're not as well insulated as residential units; they may be too heavy for your floor; they're tough to clean; and they're potentially dangerous for young children.

■ *Residential/commercial units,* a recent response to the commercial craze, were designed specifically for the home. These have the commercial look and the high BTU output but are better insulated; they also offer additional niceties such as self- or continuous-cleaning ovens.

Today's freestanding range is often the kitchen's focal point, set off by a backsplash, vent hood, or shiny pots and pans. The residential/commercial range (facing page) has custom enamel finish; here it's coupled with a brass hood and granite tile backsplash. The Southwest design at right fits range, pots, spices, and exhaust fan into a homey tiled alcove.

DESIGNER: JERRI GOLDEN

COOKTOPS

For extra flexibility, specialized needs, or simply a trim, modern look, separate cooktops make good sense. The explosive use of island and peninsula designs supports this trend.

A conventional gas or electric cooktop is built into a counter like a sink, with connections below. Unless you buy a downventing model, the unit will require an overhead hood (for more on venting, see pages 82–83). Typical units have four burners, though some have five, six, or even more.

Standard cooktop finishes include stainless steel, enameled cast iron or steel, and glass—either black or white. Sizes range from 15 to 48 inches wide, 18 to 25 inches deep, and 3 to 8 inches high (16½ inches high for downventing models).

Convertible gas or electric cooktops are similar to conventional models but offer interchangeable and reversible modules that let you replace burners with a grill, a griddle, and other specialty items.

Commercial or residential/commercial (see page 77) gas units house up to eight burners; many styles combine hot plates or griddles. Typically, these are 6 to 7 inches high with short legs for installing on a base of tile, brick, or other noncombustible material.

COMPARING COOKTOPS

Smoothtop (ceramic glass)

Electric smoothtop cooktops have burners similar to traditional coil designs but with ceramic glass on top, which disperses heat and makes the cooktop much easier to clean. In the past, these tops have received thumbs down for slow heating, but newer designs have coils closer to the surface; some models also include fast-starting coils. These units have also been slow to cool, but warning lights on some new models stay on until the top is safe to touch.

Early smoothtops also scratched or cracked, but newer formulations are more durable. Popular finishes include classic black and flecked patterns (which hide abrasions). Typically, units have three to four burners; look for independent sizing controls for smaller or larger pans. You also might be able to combine burners—to handle a large poacher, for example.

Smoothtop surfaces require flat-bottom pans for best heat dispersal.

Solid-element electric

Wander into any showroom with imported cooktops and you'll see these trim-looking burner units. They're basically cast-iron disks with resistance coils below. Because of the continuous surface, the disks produce more even heat than standard coils; and because they're sealed, they're also easier to clean.

These elements are housed in either a standard four-burner conventional top or in modules with two or three burners of different sizes. With some models, central "button" sections glow when the power is on. Better models have thermostats or on-off cycles to keep heat even and protect the unit.

Owner complaints? Solid-element burners may not produce enough heat for certain types of cooking. They also remain hot to the touch for a long time after the unit is turned off. The disks may discolor over time or with overzealous scrubbing.

Like smoothtop surfaces (discussed above), solid-element disks require flat-bottomed pans for best results.

Mix-and-match cooktop modules (often called "hobs") are the newest thing, and they're showing up everywhere. Modules, typically 12 inches wide, may be grouped together with connecting hardware or embedded separately, if you choose. Modules include standard gas, high-BTU-output gas, halogen, smoothtop electric, solid-element electric, barbecue, griddle, electric wok, or deep fryer (which some cooks use as a steamer). Some of these units fit in as little as 2 inches of vertical space, freeing up the cabinet below for drawers or a complementary oven.

Modular cooktop systems allow the cook to "mix and match" individual units; modules may be grouped together or placed individually. Shown above, from left to right, are gas, electric smoothtop, and grill units.

COMPARING COOKTOPS

Halogen

The latest technological kitchen marvel, halogen, seems the heir apparent to magnetic induction as the cutting edge of heat sources. Still more expensive to operate than gas, halogen is nonetheless the most efficient electric source; and, unlike most electric burners, halogen offers rapid on-off and infinite adjustment controls.

Halogen burners come as one of a pair of burners in 12-inch modules, or in standard four-burner set-ups combining one halogen with three standard smoothtop burners. Like other smoothtop units, many halogen cooktops now come with warning lights that stay on until the burner has completely cooled.

Halogen's weakness? It's still quite expensive—$800 to $900 per unit. The light can burn out, but it is expected to last approximately eight years before needing replacement.

Gas

Gas cooktops are the choice of most gourmet cooks; they respond instantly when turned on or off, or when settings are changed. Gas is also more economical to operate than any electric alternative.

Typical gas cooktops are 30 to 36 inches wide and feature four, five, or even six burners. Smaller modular units house two standard burners, or one standard (8,000 BTU) and one "commercial" (12,000 BTU or hotter). Pilotless ignition eliminates pilot lights, saves gas (up to 30 percent), but requires an electrical hookup.

Drawbacks? Some people find that gas smells; it may be harder to maintain than an electrical heat source. Commercial gas units may require special installation as well as heavy-duty cookware to stand up to high temperatures. Simmering can be difficult.

OVENS

Built-in ovens save counter space by hiding inside base cabinets or special vertical storage units. In separate ovens, as in cooktops, you have several choices: conventional gas or electric, microwave, and convection.

Combining a conventional radiant-heat oven with a microwave or energy-saving convection oven is a popular choice. Double ovens can be installed one above the other (with controls at eye level), or side by side below the countertop (some find this a clever use of space, others totally inefficient). You can also install a "built-under" combination unit directly below the cooktop of your choice. Your oven's interior may be "easy-off" (old-fashioned elbow grease required), continuous (a steady, slow process), or self-cleaning (the most effective method).

Radiant-heat ovens

Conventional radiant-heat ovens are available in single or double units. Single ovens range from 25 to 32 inches high and 23 to 28½ inches deep (you'll probably need extra depth for venting). The most common width is 27 inches, though many

DESIGNER: JULIE ATWOOD DESIGN

Double wall ovens (left) deliver multiple cooking options and slide neatly into an end-of-run oven cabinet; they're flanked by matching warming trays. A built-under oven (above) provides a range effect without interrupting countertop; add the cooktop of your choice.

Locate a microwave where you'll use it most: in the cooking center; near the refrigerator; or, as shown at top right, adjacent to a breakfast counter. The same rule goes for small built-ins; the toaster shown below right pops out of the backsplash area.

"space-efficient" European imports are 24 inches; recently, the 30-inch oven has also caught on. Even one 36-inch unit is available.

You can choose to include built-in warmer shelves, rotisseries, attached meat thermometers, variable-speed broilers, multiple-rack systems, pizza inserts, digital clock and timing devices, and decorator colors.

Microwave ovens

Foods cook quickly with high-frequency microwaves, but they seldom brown. Some models offer a separate browning element; other units combine microwave with radiant and/or convection cooking. Sizes range from 13 to 17 inches high, 22 to 27 inches wide, and 17 to 22 inches deep. Most units are hinged on the left.

Microwaves can be placed on a counter, built into cabinetry, or purchased as part of a double wall oven or double oven range. Some models, specially designed to be installed above a range (underneath wall cabinets), incorporate a vent and cooking lights; these are wider (30 inches) and shallower (13 to 17 inches deep). Some designers frown on the over-the-cooktop placement because it's potentially hazardous. You might even consider two microwaves—one small, portable unit near the refrigerator for quick cooking, the second in a bank of wall ovens.

Features include memory bank, programmable cooking, timers, temperature probe, rotisserie, and electronic sensors (these automatically calculate cooking time and power levels).

DESIGNER: KITCHENS BY STEWART

Convection ovens

Gas or electric convection ovens circulate hot air around the oven cavity. (You can tell them by the fan.) More energy-efficient than radiant-heat ovens, they cut cooking time by 30 percent and use reduced temperatures.

Unlike those from the microwave oven, convection-cooked foods do brown, and nicely at that. Convection is excellent for roasting and baking (it first caught on in commercial bakeries) but is less effective for foods cooked in deep or covered dishes (cakes, stews, casseroles).

Convection units vary from microwave size to standard radiant-heat size.

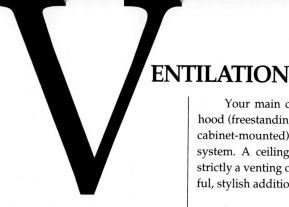ENTILATION

Installing a kitchen without planning for proper ventilation is akin to lighting a fire in the fireplace without opening the flue. The system you choose must tackle smoke, heat, grease, moisture, and odors, while remaining as quiet as possible (8 sones or less). Vent units range from totally discreet to bold and flashy.

Your main choice is between a hood (freestanding, wall-attached, or cabinet-mounted) and a downdraft system. A ceiling fan, although not strictly a venting option, can be a useful, stylish addition.

Vent hoods

Unless your range is downvented, you'll need a hood over the cooktop. Ducted hoods channel air outside; roof- or wall-mounted exterior blowers are the best blend of quiet operation and efficiency. If exterior venting is impossible, ductless hoods draw out some smoke and grease through charcoal filters.

A hood should cover the entire cooking area and extend 3 to 6 inches on each side; place its bottom edge 21 to 30 inches above the cooking surface. Commercial ranges (see page 77) and cooktops really crank out the heat: you'll need to make extra provisions for these.

Downdraft systems

If your kitchen style is open and orderly, you may wish to substitute a downdraft system in the range or

DESIGNER: BERNADINE LEACH/KITCHENS BY DESIGN

A vent hood not only provides an exit route for smoke, heat, and grease: it can look great, too. This elegant stainless unit matches edgings on both main and island countertops, as well as decorative moldings at the ceiling line.

A trim overhead vent shield (bottom left) pulls out to catch heat and grease, slides back when not in use. Cooktop downdraft system (bottom right) is discreet, great for islands and peninsulas. Although not strictly a venting option, a ceiling fan (top) helps circulate air and makes a design statement, too.

cooktop—especially if the unit is housed in an island or peninsula. Standard, convertible, and modular cooktops all come with downventing options. Some have grillwork between cooktop modules or units; others run along the back (more common with ranges). The downdraft unit sets up air currents that draw smoke, heat, and moisture down; grease is trapped below.

Are there drawbacks? Downvents don't work as well on a tall stockpot as on a skillet at cooktop level. There have been problems with long, twisted duct runs, but recent systems are more efficient than those available just a few years ago. Always route a downdraft system to the closest outside wall (see the drawing at right).

What size do you need?

The power of a fan or blower is rated in cubic feet per minute (CFM). To find the minimum acceptable number of CFM for your space, the formula is:

cubic feet x 15 ÷ 60

Figure cubic feet by multiplying width times length times height (in feet). Multiply this figure by 15, the minimum recommendation for air exchanges per hour. Then divide by 60 (minutes) to get the *minimum* acceptable CFM rating for your hood. If your cooking center is on an island or peninsula, multiply the result again by 1½ times.

Two overhead options for routing duct from a vent hood: take the direct route up through the cabinet, ceiling, and attic (A); or run it horizontally over wall cabinets in a soffit (B). Downventing is another choice: run the duct through base cabinets or below the floor (C).

Three Paths for a Vent Duct

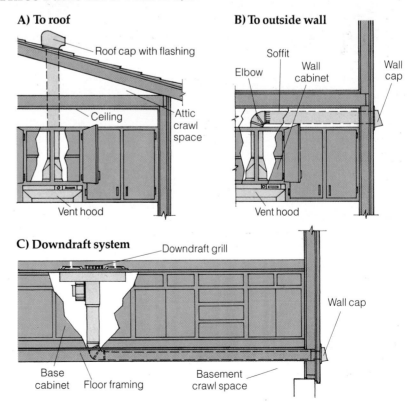

A) To roof
Roof cap with flashing
Ceiling
Attic crawl space
Vent hood

B) To outside wall
Soffit
Elbow
Wall cabinet
Wall cap
Vent hood

C) Downdraft system
Downdraft grill
Base cabinet
Floor framing
Basement crawl space
Wall cap

REFRIGERATORS

Refrigerators come in three basic versions: freestanding, built-in, and undercounter. Standard refrigerators measure from 27 to 32 inches deep, so they stand out from 24-inch-deep base cabinets. Gaining popularity are the relatively expensive 24-inch "built-ins;" most models offer interchangeable door panels to blend better with a cabinet run.

Consider these features: number of shelves, humidity drawers, meat storage compartments, temperature controls, defrosting method, ice-maker and water dispenser, convenience door, and energy-saving devices such as a power-saver switch.

Popular two- or three-door, side-by-side refrigerators permit easy visibility and access to food, but their relatively narrow shelves make it difficult to store bulky items. Other two-door models have the freezer positioned at the unit's top or bottom; the bottom mount makes it easier to reach the more often-used refrigerator sections.

Eight cubic feet of refrigerator space is recommended for two people; add a cubic foot for each additional family member and 2 extra feet if you entertain frequently. Two cubic feet per person is the rule for a freezer compartment. Typical capacities are 18.7 to 27.6 cubic feet for side-by-side refrigerators; 12 to 32 cubic feet for top-mount models; and 16.2 to 22 feet for bottom-mounts.

Undercounter refrigerators, handy for a specialty cooking center or separate entertainment area, are 33 to 34 inches high, 18 to 57 inches wide, and 25 to 32 inches deep, with a 2.5- to 6-cubic foot capacity.

DESIGNER; JULIE ATWOOD DESIGN

Organization is the byword in refrigerators. At left, faux painting, stenciling, and wrap-around niches add country charm to a glass-doored, commercial refrigerator. The view inside the built-in unit above shows a well-orchestrated system of shelves, bins, and racks. Be sure, when choosing, that you can store bulky items as needed.

DISHWASHERS & TRASH COMPACTORS

More often than not, today's cleanup centers include both a dishwasher and trash compactor—one on either side of the main sink. Here are some shopping tips.

Dishwashers

Whether portable or built-in, most dishwashers are standard size: roughly 24 inches wide, 24 inches deep, and 34 inches high. One manufacturer offers a compact 18-inch-wide built-in or portable unit; another has an undersink model for small spaces. Standard finishes include enameled steel (usually white, black, or almond), black glass, or replaceable panels to match base cabinet runs.

Quiet is the name of the game in dishwashers: improved insulation has led to operating levels as low as 50 dB. Look for such energy-saving devices as a booster heater that raises the water temperature for the dishwasher only, separate cycles for lightly or heavily soiled dishes, and air-drying options. Other features include a delay start that allows you to wash dishes at a preset time (during the night instead of at peak-energy hours), prerinse and postscrubbing cycles, a strainer filtering system (actually like a small disposer), and adjustable and/or removable racks.

Trash compactors

Compactors reduce bulky trash such as cartons, cans, and bottles to a fourth of the original size. A normal compacted load—a week's worth of trash from a family of four—will weigh 20 to 28 pounds.

Features include reversible manual or automatic doors, a separate top-bin door for loading small items (even while the unit is operating), drop-down or tilt-out drawers for easy bag removal, and a charcoal-activated filter or deodorizer to control odor. Also look for such features as a toe-operated door latch and key-activated safety switch. Sizes vary from 12 to 18 inches wide (15 inches is standard), 18 to 24½ inches deep, and 34 to 36 inches high.

Remember that a compactor is for dry, clean trash only—you'll still have to do some sorting.

The ultraquiet dishwasher at right has three tiers of rack space, including a removable flatware tray. A typical cleanup center is shown below: dishwasher and trash compactor flank main sink, facing panels blend with surrounding cabinets.

FLOORING

Two primary requirements for a kitchen floor are moisture resistance and durability. Resilient sheet flooring, ceramic tile, and properly sealed masonry or hardwood all make good candidates. Resilient flooring is the simplest (and usually the least expensive) of the four to install; the other three are trickier. And don't rule out carpeting, especially newer stain-resistant, industrial versions.

Planning checkpoints

Confused, by the array of flooring types available today? For help, study the guide below. Also, it's a good idea to visit flooring suppliers and home improvement centers; most dealers are happy to provide samples.

Beyond aesthetic considerations, you should weigh the physical char-

---

COMPARING FLOORING

Resilient

Advantages. Generally made from solid vinyl, rubber (shown at right), or polyurethane, resilients are flexible, moisture- and stain-resistant, easy to install, and simple to maintain. Another advantage is the seemingly endless variety of colors, textures, patterns, and styles available. Tiles can be mixed to form custom patterns or provide color accents.

Sheets run up to 12 feet wide, eliminating the need for seaming in some kitchens; tiles are generally 12 inches square. Vinyl and rubber are comfortable to walk on. Polyurethane finish eliminates the need for waxing.

Disadvantages. Resilients are relatively soft, making them vulnerable to dents and tears; often, though, such damage can be repaired. Tiles may collect moisture between seams if improperly installed. Some vinyl still comes with a photographically applied pattern, but most is inlaid; the latter is more expensive but wears much better.

Cost. Vinyl is least expensive. It's a good do-it-yourself project if your kitchen shape is simple; tiles are often easier to lay than sheet goods.

Ceramic tile

Advantages. Made from hard-fired slabs of clay, ceramic tile is available in dozens of patterns, colors, shapes, and finishes. Its durability, easy upkeep, and attractiveness are definite advantages.

Tiles are usually classified as *quarry tile,* commonly unglazed (unfinished) red-clay tiles that are rough and water-resistant; *pavers,* rugged unglazed tiles in earthtone shades; and *glazed tile,* available in glossy, matte, or textured finishes and in many colors.

Tile sizes run the gamut of widths, lengths, and thicknesses: by mixing sizes and colors, creative tile workers can fashion a wide range of border treatments and field accents.

Disadvantages. Tile can be cold, noisy, and, if glazed, slippery underfoot. If not properly grouted, tiles can leak moisture; some tiles will stain unless properly sealed. Grout spaces can be tough to keep clean.

Cost. Tile can cost from about $1 per square foot to nearly $40, uninstalled. Those with three-dimensional patterns and multicolored glazes can easily double costs. Purer clays fired at higher temperatures generally make costlier but better wearing tiles.

---

acteristics of flooring materials. Kitchen floors take a lot of wear and tear. Is your choice water-resistant, durable, and easy to maintain? Is it hard to walk on, noisy, or slippery underfoot?

What about subflooring?

Don't make any final flooring decision until you know the kind and condition of the subfloor your new flooring will cover.

With proper preparation, a concrete slab can serve as a base for almost any type of flooring. Other subfloors are more flexible and not suitable for rigid materials such as masonry and ceramic tile unless they are built up with extra underlayment or floor framing. Too many layers underneath can make the kitchen floor awkwardly higher than surrounding rooms. Be sure to check with a building professional or a flooring dealer for specifics.

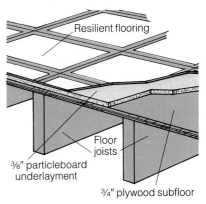

Solid, smooth support is crucial to a successful flooring job.

COMPARING FLOORING

Hardwood

Advantages. A classic hardwood floor creates a warm decor, feels good underfoot, resists wear, and can be refinished. Oak is most common; maple, birch, and beech are also available.

The three basic types are *strip,* narrow tongue-and-groove boards in random lengths; *plank,* tongue-and-groove boards in various widths and random lengths; and *wood tile,* often laid in blocks or squares, often in parquet fashion. "Floating" floor systems (one is shown at right) have several veneered strips atop each tongue-and-groove backing board. Wood flooring may be factory-prefinished or unfinished, so that it can be sanded and finished in place. Most floors can be refinished; floating systems cannot.

Disadvantages. Moisture damage and inadequate floor substructure are two bugaboos. Maintenance is another issue: some surfaces can be mopped, some cannot. Bleaching and some staining processes may wear unevenly and are difficult to repair.

Cost. From $7.50 to $13 per square foot, installed, depending on type, quality, and finish. Floating systems are generally most expensive.

Stone

Advantages. Natural stone, such as slate, flagstone, marble, granite, and limestone, has been used as flooring for centuries. Today, its use is even more practical, thanks to the development of sealers and finishes. Easy to maintain, masonry flooring is also virtually indestructible.

Stone can be used in its natural shape or cut into uniform pieces—rectangular blocks or more formal tiles. Generally, uniform pieces are butted tightly together; irregular flagstone requires grouted joints.

Man-made masonry products, specifically heat-retaining brick, are also an option for indoor use. Even colored or textured concrete can be used for finish flooring.

Disadvantages. The cost of most masonry flooring is high. Moreover, the weight of the materials requires a very strong, well-supported subfloor. Some stone—marble in particular—is cold and slippery underfoot. Careful sealing is a must; certain stones, such as limestone or granite, absorb stains and dirt readily.

Cost. From $3 per square foot for slate to $30 and over for granite.

W ALLS & CEILINGS

Adrift in the happy haze of choosing cabinets and appliances, many homeowners forget to plan for wall and ceiling treatments. Yet these surfaces go a long way toward defining the overall impact of your kitchen. Below, we'll take a brief look at your options.

Wall coverings

In addition to the backsplash areas (see page 72), your kitchen will probably include a good bit of wall space. Here are seven popular treatments.

Paint. Of course, everybody thinks of paint first, but what's best for the kitchen? Your basic choices are latex and alkyd paint.

Latex is easy to work with, and best of all, you can clean up wet paint with soap and water. Alkyd paint (often called oil-base paint) provides high gloss and will hang on a little harder than latex; however, alkyds are harder to apply and require cleanup with mineral spirits.

In general, high resin content is the mark of durable, abrasion-resistant, flexible paint—the kind you need in a kitchen. Usually, the higher the resin content the higher the gloss, so look for products labeled *gloss* or *semi-gloss* if you want a tough, washable finish.

An excellent choice for kitchen cabinets and woodwork is interior/ exterior, quick-drying alkyd enamel;

Faux-finished walls and ceiling (facing page), plus wall and floor stenciling, help integrate a 1937-vintage range with modern granite and pendant lights. The remodeled kitchen at right is linked to great-room addition via exposed beams and pitched ceiling; skylight and soffit uplighting help brighten things up.

it has a brilliant, tilelike finish that's extremely durable.

Stenciling. Stenciling, a traditional form of wall decoration, is regaining some of its former popularity, even as it takes on some modern interpretations. You can pick up a pattern or the colors from draperies, upholstery, or ceramic tiles, or you can create your own design.

Faux finishing. Faux (or, literally speaking, *false*) finishes produce in paint the appearance of other patterns or textures.

In one version, many closely related pastels are built up in subtle layers with brush strokes, by stippling, or with a sponge. Other faux finishes are bolder—including layers of textured paint and/or contrasting colors to mimic anything from traditional wallpaper to modern art.

Wallpaper. A wallpaper for the kitchen should be scrubbable, durable, and stain resistant. Solid vinyl wallpapers, available in a wide variety of colors and textures, fill the bill.

Plaster. The textured, uneven, and slightly rounded edges of plaster give a kitchen a custom, informal feel; plaster is especially popular for Southwest theme kitchens. The only

ARCHITECT: RUSHTON/CHARTOCK

& CEILINGS

drawback: The surface, if too irregular, is hard to keep clean.

Wood. Tongue-and-groove wood paneling—natural, stained, bleached, or painted—provides a charming accent to country design schemes. Wainscoting is most popular, sepa-

rated from wallpaper or paint above by the traditional chair rail.

Glass block. If you're looking for some ambient daylight but don't want to lose your privacy to a window, consider another oldtimer—glass block. These masonry units produce a soft, filtered light that complements many kitchen designs.

Ceiling treatments

Don't worry—you needn't be stuck with that old acoustic ceiling or fluorescent panel. Here's a brief survey of your alternatives.

Open it up. If your one-story house has an attic or crawl space above, you may be able to remove ceiling joists—or add more widely spaced beams—and forgo the ceiling material. Track lights and hanging pendants are popular accompaniments. You'll need to finish off the underside of the roof decking, either with tongue-and-groove wood planks or with drywall and paint. And, of course, this is the perfect time to add a skylight for extra light.

Add hollow beams. Certain kitchen styles—for example, French country—incorporate patterned beams and enclosed ceiling bays (usually painted drywall). The hollow beams are built up from 2-by lumber and molding, and provide a bonus: the inner raceways are efficient spots to hide electrical and plumbing lines or heating ducts.

Lower it. A bumpy or worn-out surface, glaring ceiling panels, or a too-tall space can all be remedied in one of two ways. Where there is no framework, first install horizontal ceiling joists; then apply a new drywall ceiling and finish it as you wish. Or nail 1-by "furring strips" over an existing ceiling, then add drywall as before.

Size up the soffits. Remember that you have several choices in the soffit space between wall cabinets and ceiling. An open soffit makes a nice display nook or can house uplighting to "lift" a ceiling. Or you might emphasize vertical lines by filling the space with taller-than-average wall cabinets. Or enclose the area with drywall or molded plaster, perhaps extending the soffits past the cabinet fronts and adding recessed downlights (see pages 91–93).

DESIGNER: DAVID SKOMSVOLD

Blue-and-white pinstriped wallpaper (above) adds subtle accent to kitchen's end wall and open soffits. Plastered soffit shelves (left) are home to colorful turtles and other Mexican collectibles.

DESIGNER: DAVID SKOMSVOLD

LIGHT FIXTURES

Today's designers separate lighting into three categories: task, ambient, and accent. Task lighting illuminates a particular area where a visual activity—such as slicing stir-fry vegetables—takes place. Ambient, or general, lighting fills in the undefined areas of a room with a soft level of light—enough, say, to munch a midnight snack by. Primarily decorative, accent lighting is used to highlight architectural features, to set a mood, or to provide drama.

What fixtures are best?

Generally speaking, *small* and *discreet* are the bywords in kitchen light fixtures; consequently, recessed downlights are by far the most popular choice in today's kitchens. Fitted with the right baffle or shield, these fixtures alone can handle ambient, task, and accent needs. Typically, downlights follow countertops or shine on the sink or island. Track lights or mono-spots also offer pinpoint task lighting or can be aimed at a wall to provide a wash of ambient light.

In addition, designers frequently tuck task lighting behind a valance under wall cabinets and over countertops. And just for fun, why not consider decorative strip lights in the kickspace area or soffit?

Surface-mounted fixtures, once a kitchen mainstay, are now used specifically to draw attention. Hanging pendants are especially popular:

While downlights are number one in kitchens, these three fixture types are also popular. A track fixture (upper left) shines down from ceiling soffit; an undercabinet strip (upper right) lights up the countertop; decorative pendants (right) illuminate the island and dining area.

place them over a breakfast nook or an island—or anywhere else they won't present a hazard.

Dimmers (also called rheostats) enable you to set a fixture or group of fixtures at any level from a soft glow to a radiant brightness. They're also energy savers.

DESIGNER: OSBURN DESIGN

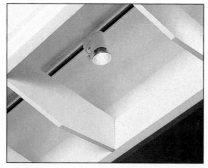

Light bulbs & tubes

Light sources can be grouped in general categories according to the way they produce light.

Incandescent light. This light, the kind used most frequently in our homes, is produced by a tungsten

DESIGNER: KITCHENS BY STEWART

thread that burns slowly inside a glass bulb. A-bulbs are the old standbys; R and PAR bulbs produce a more controlled beam; silvered-bowl types diffuse light. A number of decorative bulbs are also available.

Low-voltage incandescent lighting is especially useful for accent lighting. Operating on 12 or 24 volts, these lights require transformers (which are often built into the fixtures) to step down the voltage from standard 120-volt household circuits.

Fluorescent light. Fluorescent tubes are unrivaled for energy efficiency; they also last far longer than incandescent bulbs. In some energy-conscious areas, general lighting for new kitchens *must* be fluorescent.

Older fluorescent tubes have been criticized for noise, flicker, and poor color rendition. Electronic ballasts and better fixture shielding against glare have remedied the first two problems; as for the last one, manufacturers have developed fluorescents in a wide spectrum of colors, from very warm (about 2,700 degrees K) to very cool (about 6,300 degrees K).

Quartz halogen. These bright, white newcomers are excellent for task lighting, pinpoint accenting, and other dramatic accents. Halogen is usually low-voltage but may be standard line current. The popular MR-16 bulb creates the tightest beam; for a longer reach and wider coverage, choose a PAR bulb. There's an abundance of smaller bulb shapes and sizes that fit pendants and under-cabinet strip lights.

Halogen has two disadvantages: high initial cost and its very high heat. Be sure to shop carefully: some fixtures on the market are not UL-approved.

Light fixtures really shine in this all low-voltage halogen kitchen. Wire-suspended spots and cones provide ambient light; downlights over the sink add both task lighting and decorative accents; under-cabinet strips light up countertops and backsplashes.

COMPARING LIGHT BULBS & TUBES

INCANDESCENT

A-bulb
Description. Familiar pear shape; frosted or clear.
Uses. Everyday household use.

T—Tubular
Description. Tube-shaped, from 5" long. Frosted or clear.
Uses. Appliances, cabinets, decorative fixtures.

R—Reflector
Description. White or silvered coating directs light out end of funnel-shaped bulb.
Uses. In directional fixtures; focuses light where needed.

PAR—Parabolic aluminized reflector
Description. Similar to auto headlamp; special shape and coating project light and control beam.
Uses. In recessed downlights and track fixtures.

Silvered bowl
Description. A-bulb, with silvered cap to cut glare and produce indirect light.
Uses. In track fixtures and pendants.

Low-voltage strip lights
Description. Like Christmas tree lights; in strips or tracks, or encased in flexible, waterproof plastic.
Uses. Task lighting and decoration.

FLUORESCENT

Tube
Description. Tube-shaped, 5" to 96" long. Needs special fixture and ballast.
Uses. Shadowless work light; also indirect lighting.

PL—Compact tube
Description. U-shaped with base; 5¼" to 7½" long.
Uses. In recessed downlights; some PL tubes include ballasts to replace A-bulbs.

QUARTZ HALOGEN

High-intensity
Description. Small, clear bulb with consistently high light output; used in halogen fixtures.
Uses. In specialized task lamps, torchères, and pendants.

Low-voltage MR-16 (mini-reflector)
Description. Tiny (2"-diameter) projector bulb; gives small circle of light from a distance.
Uses. In low-voltage track fixtures, mono-spots, and recessed downlights.

Low-voltage PAR
Description. Similar to auto headlight; tiny filament, shape, and coating give precise direction.
Uses. To project a small spot of light a long distance.

INFORMATION SOURCES

When you're transforming an old kitchen into one that's innovative and workable, you'll find a wealth of ideas and information in brochures put out by the various manufacturers listed on these pages. They can also tell you about local outlets and distributors for their products. The addresses and phone numbers in this list are accurate as of press time.

The yellow pages of your telephone directory and the National Kitchen & Bath Association (124 Main Street, Hackettstown, NJ 07840) can help you locate kitchen showrooms, cabinetmakers, designers, architects, and other sources near you.

APPLIANCES

ABBAKA
435 23rd Street
San Francisco, CA 94107
415-648-7210

AEG
ANDI-CO. Appliances
65 Campus Plaza
Edison, NJ 08837
201-225-8837

AGA Cookers
Cooper & Turner, Inc.
R.F.D. 1, Box 477
Stowe, VT 05672
802-253-9729

Admiral Co.
Maycor Corp.
240 Edwards
Cleveland, TN 37311
615-472-3333

Amana Refrigeration, Inc.
Highway 220
Amana, IA 52204
319-622-5511

ASEA Dishwashers
ASKO Inc.
903 Bowser Street #170
Richardson, TX 75081
1-800-367-2444

Casablanca Fan Co.
PO Box 424
City of Industry, CA 91747
818-369-6441

Creda
1-800-99-CREDA

Dacor
950 S. Raymond Avenue
Pasadena, CA 91109
818-799-1000

Euroflair/Frigidaire
WCI Appliance Group
6000 Perimeter Drive
Dublin, OH 43017
1-800-451-7007

Gaggenau USA Corp.
425 University Avenue
Norwood, MA 02062
617-255-1766

GE/Hotpoint Appliances
General Electric Co.
Appliance Park
Louisville, KY 40225
800-626-2000

In-Sink-Erator
Emerson Electric Company
4700 21st Street
Racine, WI 53406
800-558-5712

Jenn-Air Co.
3035 N. Shadeland Avenue
Indianapolis, IN 46226
317-545-2271

KitchenAid, Inc.
701 Main Street
St. Joseph, MI 49085
616-982-4500

La Cornue Range
Purcell-Murray Co.
113 Park Lane
Brisbane, CA 94005
800-892-4040

Miele Appliances, Inc.
22D Worlds Fair Drive
Somerset, NJ 08873
201-560-0899

Modern Maid
403 N. Main Street
Topton, PA 19562
215-682-4211

NuTone, Inc.
Madison & Red Bank Roads
Cincinnati, OH 45227
513-527-5100

Sub-Zero Freezer Co.
PO Box 4130
Madison, WI 53711
608-271-2233

Thermador
5119 District Boulevard
Los Angeles, CA 90040
213-562-1133

Traulsen & Co., Inc.
114-02 15th Avenue
College Point, NY 11356
718-463-9000

Viking Range Corp.
PO Box 8012
Greenwood, MS 38930
601-455-1200

Whirlpool Corp.
2000 M63 North
Benton Harbor, MI 49022
800-253-1301

White-Westinghouse
4007 Paramount Boulevard,
Suite 100
Lakewood, CA 90712
800-421-2972
800-262-1969 (Calif)

Wolf Range Co.
19600 S. Alameda Street
PO Box 7050
Compton, CA 90224
213-774-7565

CABINETS

Allmilmö Corp.
70 Clinton Road
Fairfield, NJ 07004
201-227-2502

Dura Supreme
300 Dura Drive
Howard Lake, MN 55349
612-543-3872

Kraftmaid
16052 Industrial Parkway
Middlefield, OH 44062
216-632-5333

Merillat Industries, Inc.
5353 W, US 223
Adrian, MI 49221
517-263-0771

Poggenpohl USA Corp.
5905 Johns Road
Tampa, FL 33634
813-882-9292

Quaker Maid
WCI, Inc.
Route 61
Leesport, PA 19533
215-926-3011

Rutt Custom Kitchens
Route 23
Goodville, PA 17528
215-445-6751

Sears/Kenmore
Sears Tower
Department 703
Chicago, IL 60684
312-875-2500

SieMatic
One Neshaminy Interplex
Suite 207
Trevose, PA 19047
215-244-0700

**Smallbone Traditional
English Kitchens**
150 E. 58th Street
Suite 904
New York, NY 10155
212-935-3222

Snaidero West, Inc.
Pacific Design Center
8687 Melrose Avenue B487
Los Angeles, CA 90069
213-854-0222

Wm Ohs Cabinets
5095 Peoria Street
Denver, CO 80239
303-371-6550

Wood-Mode Cabinetry
Wood Metal Industries
One Second Street
Kreamer, PA 17833
717-374-2711

COUNTERTOPS

American Olean Tile Co., Inc.
PO Box 271
Lansdale, PA 19446
215-855-1111

Avonite, Inc.
5100 Goldleaf Circle
Suite 200
Los Angeles, CA 90056
800-4-AVONITE
800-428-6648 (Calif)

Color Tile
See listing for FLOORING

Corian Building Products
E. I. DuPont de Nemours
& Co.
1007 Market Street
Wilmington, DE 19898
800-441-7515

Dal-Tile
See listing for FLOORING

Formica Corp.
One Stanford Road
PO Box 338
Piscataway, NJ 08854
201-469-1555

Nevamar Corp.
8339 Telegraph Road
Odenton, MD 21113
301-551-5000

Summitville Tiles, Inc.
Summitville, OH 43962
216-223-1511

Wilsonart
Ralph Wilson Plastics Co.
600 General Bruce Drive
Temple, TX 76501
800-433-3222
800-792-6000 (Texas)

FLOORING

American Olean Tile Co., Inc.
PO Box 271
Lansdale, PA 19446
215-855-1111

Armstrong World Industries, Inc.
PO Box 3001
Lancaster, PA 17604
800-233-3823

Bruce Hardwood Floors
PO Box 660100
Dallas, TX 75266-0100
214-931-3000

Color Tile
PO Box 2475
Fort Worth, TX 76113
817-870-9400

Congoleum Corp.
861 Sloan Avenue
Trenton, NJ 08619
609-584-3000

Dal-Tile
7834 Hawn Freeway
Dallas, TX 75217
214-398-1411

Mannington Mills, Inc.
PO Box 30
Salem, NJ 08079
609-935-3000

Summitville Tiles, Inc.
Summitville, OH 43962
216-223-1511

LIGHT FIXTURES

Casablanca Fan Co.
PO Box 424
City of Industry, CA 91747
818-369-6441

Halo Lighting
6842 Walker Street
La Palma, CA 90623
714-522-7171

Hunter Fan Co.
2500 Frisco Avenue
Memphis, TN 38114
901-743-1360

Lightolier/Genlyte
100 Lighting Way
Secaucus, NJ 07096-1508
201-864-3000

Progress Lighting
Erie Avenue & G Street
Philadelphia, PA 19134
215-289-1200

SINKS & FITTINGS

ABBAKA
435 23rd Street
San Francisco, CA 94107
415-648-7210

American Standard, Inc.
U.S. Plumbing Products
PO Box 6820
Piscataway, NJ 08855
201-980-3000

Blanco Sinks
Western States Manufacturing Corp.
1559 Sunland Lane
Costa Mesa, CA 92626
714-557-1933

The Chicago Faucet Co.
2100 S. Nuclear Drive
Des Plaines, IL 60018
312-694-4400

Culligan International Co.
One Culligan Parkway
Northbrook, IL 60062
708-205-6000

Delta Faucet Co.
55 E. 11th Street
PO Box 40980
Indianapolis, IN 46280
317-848-1812

Eljer
PO Box 869037
Plano, TX 75086-9037
214-881-7177

Elkay Manufacturing
2222 Camden Court
Oak Brook, IL 60521
708-574-8484

Everpure Filtration Systems
660 N. Blackhawk Drive
Westmont, IL 60559
312-654-4000

Franke, Inc.
Kitchen Systems Division
Box 428
Hatfield, PA 19440
800-626-5771

Grohe America, Inc.
900 Lively Boulevard
Wood Dale, IL 60191
708-350-2600

In-Sink-Erator Division
Emerson Electric Co.
4700 21st Street
Racine, WI 53406
800-558-5712

Jenn-Air Co.
3035 Shadeland
Indianapolis, IN 46226
317-545-2271

KitchenAid Inc.
701 Main Street
St. Joseph, MI 49085
616-982-4500

Kohler Co.
444 Highland Drive
Kohler, WI 53044
414-457-4441

KWC Faucets
Western States Manufacturing Corp.
1559 Sunland Lane
Costa Mesa, CA 92626
714-557-1933

Luwa Corp.
PO Box 16348
Charlotte, NC 28297
704-394-8341

Porcher Sinks
650 Maple Avenue
Torrance, CA 90503
213-212-6112

STORAGE PRODUCTS

Closet Maid
Clairson International
720 SW 17th Street
Ocala, FL 32674
904-351-6100

Elfa/Eurica Marketing, Inc.
1760 East Wilshire Avenue
Santa Ana, CA 92705-4615
714-285-1000

Iron-A-Way, Inc.
220 W. Jackson
Morton, IL 61550
309-266-7232

Rev-a-Shelf, Inc.
2409 Plantside Drive
PO Box 99585
Jefferson, KY 40299
800-626-1126
502-499-5835

Rubbermaid Inc.
1147 Akron Rd.
Wooster, OH 44691
216-264-6464

INDEX

In addition to the references below, see pages 22–59 for designs, materials, and equipment as used in finished kitchens.